Samuel Taylor Coleridge

Selected and edited by JOHN BEER

University of Cambridge

WEIDENFELD & NICOLSON

First published in 1996 by J M Dent
This edition published in 2023 by Weidenfeld & Nicolson
An imprint of The Orion Publishing Group Ltd
Carmelite House
50 Victoria Embankment
London EC4Y 0DZ

An Hachette UK Company

1 3 5 7 9 10 8 6 4 2

A CIP catalogue record for this book
is available from the British Library.

ISBN (mmp) 978 1 3996 1415 3
ISBN (ebook) 978 1 7802 2314 8

Printed in the UK by Clays Ltd, Elcograf S.p.A.

www.orionbooks.co.uk
www.weidenfeldandnicolson.co.uk

Contents

Note on the Author and Editor   v
Chronology of Coleridge's Life and Times   vi
Introduction   xvi

Poems

On the Prospect of Establishing a Pantisocracy in America   3
Pantisocracy   3
To the Rev. W. L. Bowles   4
Lines (composed while climbing the left ascent of Brockley
   Coomb)   4
The Eolian Harp   5
Reflections on Having Left a Place of Retirement   7
This Lime-Tree Bower my Prison   9
Sonnets Attempted in the Manner of Contemporary Writers   12
Frost at Midnight   14
Lewti   16
The Nightingale   19
The Ballad of the Dark Ladié   22
Kubla Khan   24
The Rime of the Ancient Mariner   27
France: An Ode   48
Fears in Solitude   51
Christabel   57
Love   76
To Mr Pye   80
To a Critic   80
Letter to – [Sara Hutchinson]   81
Hymn before Sun-Rise, in the Vale of Chamouni   90

The Pains of Sleep   93
Phantom   94
Constancy to an Ideal Object   95
[The Indifference of the Heavens]   96
Recollections of Love   97
A Tombless Epitaph   98
Limbo   99
Song (from *Zapolya*)   100
Work Without Hope   101
The Pang More Sharp Than All   101
Song   103
Love's Apparition and Evanishment   104
Epitaph   105

Note on the Author and Editor

SAMUEL TAYLOR COLERIDGE was born on 21 July 1772 at Ottery St Mary in Devon. After being educated at Christ's Hospital in London and Jesus College, Cambridge he worked as an independent writer, speaker and thinker, producing his first collection of poems in 1796 and enlarging it in 1797. Close collaboration with Wordsworth in north Somerset resulted in joint production of the volume *Lyrical Ballads* in 1798 and stimulated his poetic powers more generally: this period saw poems as diverse as 'Frost at Midnight', 'Kubla Khan' and the unfinished 'Christabel'. After wintering in Germany in 1797–8 he settled, like Wordsworth, in the Lake District, where he wrote the 'Letter' that he turned into 'Dejection: An Ode' (1802), a fruit of his hopeless love for Wordsworth's sister-in-law Sara Hutchinson and the growing unhappiness of his marriage. The poem also signalled fears about the continuance of his creativity, but although he now turned increasingly to prose, writing on politics (*Essays on his Own Times* and *Lay Sermons*), criticism (Lectures on Shakespeare and *Biographia Literaria* (1817)) and religion (*Aids to Reflection* (1825) and *On the Constitution of the Church and State* (1829)), and planning a great new philosophical work, poetry continued to flow. After going to live with the Gillmans at Highgate in 1816, he published *Sibylline Leaves* (1817), containing revisions of his earlier poems and new ones such as 'Limbo' and 'Ne plus Ultra'. Further collections followed and new poems (some looking back wistfully to his early life) continued to appear in most years until his death in 1834.

JOHN BEER'S work on Coleridge includes two books, *Coleridge the Visionary* and *Coleridge's Poetic Intelligence*, the editing of a collection of bicentenary essays, *Coleridge's Variety*, and the preparation of an edition of *Aids to Reflection* for Coleridge's *Collected Works*. He is also general editor of the series *Coleridge's Writings* and has written on a variety of other authors, including books on Blake, Wordsworth and E. M. Forster.

Chronology of Coleridge's Life

Year	Age	Life
1770		
1771		
1772		Born 21 October at Ottery St Mary, Devon, youngest of ten children
1774		
1775		
1776	4	
1778	6	Attends Ottery Grammar School
1779		
1780		
1781	9	Death (6 October) of Coleridge's father
1782	10	Attends Christ's Hospital, London to 1791
1783	11	
1784	12	
1785	13	
1787	15	
1788	16	Elected Grecian; meets Evans family
1789	17	

Chronology of his Times

Year	Literary Context	Historical Events
1770	Wordsworth born	
1771	Scott born	
1772		
1774	Southey born	Priestley discovers oxygen
1775	Lamb born	
1776	Smith, *Wealth of Nations*	US Declaration of Independence
	Gibbon, *Decline and Fall*	
1778	Hazlitt born	London Swedenborgians found
	Rousseau and Voltaire die	New Church
1779	Johnson, *Lives of the Poets*	
1780		The Gordon Riots
1781	Schiller, *Die Räuber*	
	Rousseau, *Confessions*	
1782		
1783	Blake, *Poetical Sketches*	Pitt's first ministry
1784	Samuel Johnson dies	
1785	De Quincey born	
	Cowper, *The Task*	
1787	Thomas Taylor, *Concerning the Beautiful* (Plotinus)	
1788	Byron born	
	Crowe, *Lewesdon Hill*	
1789	Blake, *Songs of Innocence*	Fall of Bastille (14 July); French Revolution
	Darwin, *The Botanic Garden*	

Year	Age	Life
1790	18	
1791	19	Jesus College, Cambridge, Exhibitioner, Sizar, Scholar
1792	20	Wins Browne medal with Greek Sapphic 'Ode on the Slave Trade'
1793	21	Attends Cambridge trial of William Frend. Enlists in 15th Light Dragoons as Silas Tomkyn Comberbache
1794	22	Meets Robert Southey in Oxford and plans Pantisocracy; Welsh tour. *Religious Musings* begun
1795	23	Political Lectures begin. Marriage (4 October) to Sara Fricker
1796	24	*The Watchman* and *Poems on Various Subjects*. Move to Stowey
1797	25	At Racedown (June). The Wordsworths to Alfoxden House. *Poems*. 'Kubla Khan' composed; 'Ancient Mariner' begun
1798	26	Wedgwood £150 annuity accepted. 'Frost at Midnight'. 'The Recantation', later 'France: An Ode' (March); 'Fears in Solitude'. *Lyrical Ballads*. The Wordsworths, Chester and Coleridge to Germany
1799	27	To University of Göttingen. Ascent of Brocken. Return to Stowey (July). Meets Sara Hutchinson at Sockburn (October)
1800	28	*Morning Post* reporter and leader-writer; translating *Wallenstein*
1801	29	*Lyrical Ballads* (1800) published
1802	30	'A Letter to – [Sara Hutchinson]'. 'Dejection' ode in *Morning Post*

Year	Literary Context	Historical Events
1790	Burke, *Reflections on the Revolution in France*	
1791	Paine, *Rights of Man* Boswell, *Life of Johnson*	Anti-Jacobin riots; Priestley's house attacked
1792	Rogers, *Pleasures of Memory* Wollstonecraft, *Rights of Woman*	
1793	Godwin, *Political Justice* Wordsworth, *An Evening Walk* and *Descriptive Sketches*	Louis XVI and Marie Antoinette executed; France declares war on England; Reign of Terror
1794	Paine, *Age of Reason* Radcliffe, *Udolpho* Blake, *Songs of Experience* E. Darwin, *Zoonomia*	Robespierre executed; end of Terror. State Trials: Hardy, Tooke and Thelwall acquitted
1795	Keats and Carlyle born M. G. Lewis, *The Monk* Goethe, *Wilhelm Meister*	
1796	Robert Burns dies Mary Lamb's violent illness	Threats of invasion. Jenner's first vaccination
1797	*Anti-Jacobin* begins Radcliffe, *The Italian*	Pitt proposes to finance the war against France by increasing taxes. Mutinies in British navy
1798	Lloyd, *Edmund Oliver* Malthus, *Essay on the Principles of Population*	Swiss cantons suppressed (spring). Bonaparte invades Egypt; Battle of the Nile
1799	Schiller, *Piccolomini* and *Wallensteins Tod* published	Bonaparte first consul. Royal Institution founded
1800		Fox returns to Parliament; Bill for Union passed
1801		Battle of Copenhagen
1802	Scott, *Minstrelsy of the Scottish Border* begun	Peace of Amiens

Year	Age	Life
1803	31	Scottish tour with Wordsworths
1804	32	Under-secretary at Malta
1805	33	Acting Public Secretary in Malta
1806	34	In Rome and Tuscany. Return to England (August)
1807	35	Hears Wordsworth read *Prelude*
1808	36	Lectures at Royal Institution on Poetry and Principles of Taste
1809	37	*The Friend* (1 June–15 March 1810)
1810	38	Sara Hutchinson leaves Grasmere for Wales. *The Friend* last number. Montagu precipitates Wordsworth-Coleridge quarrel
1811	39	Lectures on Shakespeare and Milton attended by Collier, Byron, Rogers, Crabb Robinson
1812	40	Lamb and Crabb Robinson patch quarrel with Wordsworth. Belles Lettres lectures in Surrey Institution. Lectures in Bristol. Illness and spiritual crisis at Bath and Bristol
1813	41	
1814	42	*Remorse* performed in Bristol. Moves with Morgans to Calne, Wiltshire
1815	43	Printing of *Sibylline Leaves* begins at Bristol

Year	Literary Context	Historical Events
1803	Malthus, *Essay on . . . Population* (2nd edn)	War declared against France
1804		Bonaparte becomes emperor
1805	Scott, *Lay of the Last Minstrel*	Trafalgar and Austerlitz
1806		'Ministry of All the Talents'
1807	Crabbe, *The Parish Register*	Bonaparte attacks Russia. Peninsular War begins
1808	John and Leigh Hunt begin *Examiner* Goethe, *Faust*, Part I	Convention of Cintra; Bonaparte invades Spain
1809	Byron, *English Bards and Scotch Reviewers*	Bonaparte captures Vienna
1810	Scott, *Lady of the Lake* Southey, *Curse of Kehama* Crabbe, *The Borough*	George III generally recognised as insane
1811	Shelley, *Necessity of Atheism* Austen, *Sense and Sensibility*	Prince of Wales made regent. Luddite uprisings begin
1812	Combe, *Tour of Dr Syntax in Search of the Picturesque* Byron, *Childe Harold*, Cantos I and II	Spencer Perceval assassinated. Bonaparte enters Russia; retreat from Moscow
1813	Austen, *Pride and Prejudice* Shelley, *Queen Mab*	Wellington enters France
1814	Wordsworth, *Excursion* Scott, *Waverley* Cary's *Dante* completed	Bonaparte abdicates, exiled to Elba; restoration of the Bourbons
1815	Wordsworth, *Poems* of 1815; *The White Doe of Rylstone*	Bonaparte escapes from Elba; the Hundred Days; Waterloo

Year	Age	Life
1816	44	Accepted as patient and house-mate by James Gillman, Surgeon, Highgate. *Christabel, Kubla Khan* and *The Pains of Sleep. Statesman's Manual*
1817	45	Second *Lay Sermon, Biographia Literaria, Sibylline Leaves, Zapolya*
1818	46	'Treatise on Method'. *The Friend,* 3-vol. edition. Lectures: on Philosophy, on Shakespeare, on Milton, Dante, Spenser, Cervantes
1819	47	Meets Keats in Millfield Lane; Hartley Coleridge elected Probationary Fellow of Oriel
1820	48	Renewed plans for Great Work; Hartley Coleridge refused renewal of fellowship
1821	49	Progress on Great Work continues
1822	50	First record (29 December) of table talk made by H. N. Coleridge
1823	51	Gillmans move to 3 The Grove, Highgate
1824	52	Carlyle calls at Highgate
1825	53	'On the *Prometheus* of Aeschylus'. *Aids to Reflection* published
1827	55	Netherlands and Rhine Tour with Wordsworths. *Poetical Works,* 3 vols
1829	57	*Poetical Works,* 2nd edn; Sara Coleridge marries H. N. Coleridge; *On the Constitution of the Church and State*

Year	Literary Context	Historical Events
1816	Shelley, *Alastor and Other Poems* Peacock, *Headlong Hall*	Byron's departure from England. Spa Fields riot
1817	*Blackwood's Magazine* founded Keats, *Poems*	Elgin Marbles purchased for British Museum
1818	Keats, *Endymion* Hazlitt, *Lectures on the English Poets* Peacock, *Nightmare Abbey* Mary Shelley, *Frankenstein*	
1819	Wordsworth, *Peter Bell* Byron, *Don Juan* (to 1824) Shelley, *Masque of Anarchy*	Peterloo massacre (16 August)
1820	Keats, *Lamia and Other Poems* Lamb, *Essays of Elia* Shelley, *Prometheus Unbound*	George III dies
1821	Keats dies in Rome De Quincey, *Confessions*	
1822	Shelley dies in Italy Byron, *Vision of Judgment*	Congress of Verona
1823	Hazlitt, *Liber Amoris*	War between France and Spain
1824		Byron dies in Greece
1825	Hazlitt, *The Spirit of the Age*	Stockton to Darlington railway opened
1827	Blake dies	
1828	Hazlitt, *Life of Napoleon* (to 1830)	
1829	Sir Humphry Davy dies	Catholic Relief Bill passed

Year	Age	Life
1830	58	*The Devil's Walk* reissued
1832	60	
1833	61	At Cambridge for meetings of British Association; Emerson calls
1834		*Poetical Works*, 3rd edn. Dies at Highgate, 25 July

Year	Literary Context	Historical Events
1830	Tennyson, *Poems*	Death of George IV
1832	Crabbe and Scott die	Reform Bill becomes law
1833	Carlyle, *Sartor Resartus* Browning, *Pauline*	Keble's Assize sermon; Oxford Movement initiated
1834	Lamb dies (27 December)	New Poor Law

Introduction

Coleridge had hopes from his earliest years that he would be remembered as a poet. As a young man, however, he was also caught up in the turbulence surrounding the French Revolution and believed that he ought to contribute to the debates and demands for action that followed it in England. Together with Robert Southey he planned to set up a small egalitarian society to be called 'Pantisocracy' on the banks of the Susquehannah. The plans proved abortive, but for some time his poetry was devoted to that and other political themes.

At the same time he realised that his chief interest was in relationships between individual human beings and in their sensibilities. For this reason the appearance in his poems of the word 'heart' (normally passed over by modern readers as a meaningless cliché) always repays close attention, as marking a moment of particular engagement. Coleridge's interest in the human heart extends to its physical workings – a fact which helps to develop the form of his poetry in a curiously apposite manner. Some years ago Albert Gérard pointed out that in many poems an effect of 'systole' and 'diastole' could be traced. The poem, in other words, begins by focusing upon some intimate and immediate scene, which is described in careful detail; it then expands to take in a wider landscape – which occasions corresponding reflections upon larger intellectual concerns – and the poem finally returns to the local and particular scene, which is now seen to be newly illuminated by all that has been said in the poem. Such a structure may not only be traced (with variations) in direct 'conversation poems', such as 'This Lime Tree Bower' and 'Frost at Midnight', but extends its influence as far as 'The Ancient Mariner', where the Mariner returns from the most expansive of voyages to his native village endowed with new knowledge and the Guest, who has accompanied him in his imagination, sees the wedding-feast to which he was going in a different light. This movement of systole and diastole (which is of course the basic motion of the human heart) could take in large emotional movements, such as dilation to sublimity and contraction to pathos, for which eighteenth-century poetry had found less room.

Coleridge's inclination to turn away from political movements and concentrate instead on the cultivation of personal relationships prompted criticism and encouragement from friends who themselves had aspirations to be poets, in particular, Charles Lamb. As early as 1794 the two friends seem to have agreed on the most important requirement of poetry. In a poem addressed to Lamb that December Coleridge wrote:

> Thus far my sterile Brain hath fram'd the song
> Elaborate & swelling – but the Heart
> Not owns it.

Nearly two years later Lamb took up the same theme:

Cultivate simplicity, Coleridge, or rather, I should say, banish elaborateness; for simplicity springs spontaneous from the heart, and carries into daylight its own modest buds and genuine, sweet, and clear flowers of expression. I allow no hot-beds in the gardens of Parnassus.

It was not until 1797, however, when William and Dorothy Wordsworth came to live near him in north Somerset, that Coleridge's poetic powers really blossomed. The Wordsworths not only shared his sense of the human heart's importance but linked it with their own experience of nature. Dorothy had an openness of heart and directness of response, both to nature and to her fellow human beings, which were unusual in that decorous age; Wordsworth brought a sensibility which had (unlike Coleridge's) remained close to wild nature throughout his most formative years. Together the three friends walked the countryside and studied nature, looking for points where she might be said to display a correspondence with human feeling. The poems composed by the two men, together with Dorothy Wordsworth's journals, make up a composite and complementary document of their aspirations: they were intent, evidently, on exploring the idea that exposure to nature might be one of the most beneficient moral resources available to man. At the same time this brought them necessarily face to face with the intractable problem of evil. So far as Coleridge is concerned, the results of the discussions appear most vividly in 'The Ancient Mariner' and 'Kubla Khan', poems which both carry some reference to the daemonic forces that seem to be particularly involved in evil behaviour. Kubla Khan is, it seems, a man of commanding genius who does not understand the full destructive power of his own creative daemon; the Ancient Mariner, by his thoughtless act in shooting an albatross, unleashes equally ambiguous daemonic forces, which continue to wreak vengeance upon him until, in a sudden uprush of the heart's imagination, he glimpses the depth and significance of what he has done; after which they demand – and assist – further penance. Similar forces play a part in 'Christabel': the Geraldine whom Christabel discovers in the forest is an ambiguous daemonic figure, acting partly for Christabel's good, partly exercising a subtly malign influence.

These were essentially experimental poems, however, and their composition posed further problems. For if one accepts the implied philosophy of 'The Ancient Mariner' – that human beings act evilly because they do not understand what they are doing – it follows that they can be redeemed from their foolish behaviour only by being taught its full implications; but if this must come about through privations such as those suffered by the Mariner, the likelihood of the mass of mankind coming to such knowledge is very small.

Coleridge's recognition of such dilemmas was accompanied by a growing crisis in his domestic life. After his return from Germany, which he visited with the Wordsworths in 1798–9, he fell in love with Sara Hutchinson, Wordsworth's sister-in-law, who apparently touched his heart in a way that his own wife had never done. The result, however, was not release, but self-contradiction. According to his own philosophy, the relationship ought to have resulted in a new upsurge of creative power, yet he found himself lapsing more and more frequently into dejection. He succeeded in adding another part to 'Christabel', but the ebullience that had characterised the poetry of 1797–8 could not be regained: at its best the poetry of the time was finely drawn, but analytic rather than resonant. Its quality is well typified in the very lines from the 'Letter to Sara Hutchinson' which express his condition:

> There *was* a time when tho' my path was rough
> The Joy within me dallied with Distress;
> And all Misfortunes were but as the Stuff
> Whence Fancy made me Dreams of Happiness;
> For Hope grew round me, like the climbing Vine,

> And Leaves & Fruitage, not my own, seem'd mine!
> But now Ill Tidings bow me down to earth
> Nor care I, that they rob me of my Mirth
>   But oh! each Visitation
> Suspends what Nature gave me at my Birth,
>   My shaping Spirit of Imagination!

The man who can write lines such as these has clearly not lost all his poetic powers, but he will find it difficult to project whole new poetic structures.

He did not give up poetry altogether but, in a number of poems written during the whole period, seems to have made up for the loss of his 'shaping spirit' by taking contemporary German poems and using some part of their structure as a starting point for creations of his own – an activity which might charitably be construed as 'priming the pump'. 'Hymn before Sun-rise', for example, the original inspiration for which, Coleridge said, came during a climb on Scafell, owes something of its form and detail to a short German poem by Friederike Brun. From her introductory note and exclamatory stanzas, which repeat the name 'Jehovah', thundered forth from mountain streams, Coleridge takes his own introductory note and pious exclamations, but constructs a larger statement, including a reference to his belief that in the contemplation of the great forms of nature the soul is transported into an excitement and self-forgetfulness by which, through a natural sympathy, it is enabled to acknowledge the divine.

The growing popularity of Coleridge's poetry during his lifetime was partly due to its influence upon his immediate successors, some of whom developed particular aspects of themes well beyond the point he had reached. Keats, for example, seems to have found in poems such as 'The Eolian Harp' and 'The Nightingale' inspiration for his poetry of warm sensuousness; Shelley was evidently encouraged by the link between natural description and metaphysical psychology (especially in the nature poetry) to develop a similar mode in his Odes. Byron, who was particularly impressed by 'Kubla Khan' developed Oriental tales of his own.

In his later years Coleridge would move towards a more radical view of his great poem: 'The Ancient Mariner', he now thought, was a 'poem' of the pure imagination' which would have been even more successful if it had been written from an amoral point of view, as in *The Arabian Nights*, where actions are often punished on the basis of some arbitrary rule that the human being who committed them could not have known or been expected to know. 'The chief fault, if I might say so, was the obtrusion of the moral sentiment so openly on the reader as a principle or cause of action in a work of such pure imagination.' To Mrs Barbauld, who claimed that the poem had no moral, he replied that on the contrary it had too much. When this comment was made is not clear; however, it should in any case be observed that in 1817 the 'moral sentiment' was being reinforced in the newly added marginal glosses, and that in his 'Epitaph', written shortly before his death, he was still voicing a hope that he might, in the grave, find 'life in death'. The inner debate concerning the exact moral significance of his poem was evidently never resolved; but since his audience increasingly agreed on the imaginative impact of the poem, he could safely dwell on this as its most distinctive achievement.

If we think of 'The Ancient Mariner' as expressing Coleridge's most central poetic voice, we are also forced to note that its accents were not simple. When his imagination is most powerfully at work, his voice is complex and dramatically rich, ranging from the judicious archaism of 'To Mary Queen the praise be given' to the dramatic alternation between the Two Voices. Nevertheless there are moments when simplicity breaks through memorably, as in the uprushing, directly enacted emotion of

> We drifted o'er the harbour-bar
> And I with sobs did pray –
> O let me be awake, my God!
> Or let me sleep away.

The most characteristic note in Coleridge's voice – that of eager delight – is never far below the surface in his most imaginative poetry.

If the voice that is heard in the later poetry is a more labouring one, it is one that remains true to Coleridge's great themes. The role of imagination was always hard to come to terms with: sometimes it seemed to have acted as a dangerous and elusive will-o'-the-wisp, sometimes it seemed to have been no less than 'the vision and the faculty divine'. But of the heart's importance, however much its movements (and the corresponding movements of his verse) might be deadened by his gradual loss of hope, he had no doubt at all.

JOHN BEER

Samuel Taylor Coleridge

On the Prospect of Establishing a Pantisocracy in America

Whilst pale Anxiety, corrosive Care,
  The Tear of Woe, the gloom of sad Despair,
  And deepen'd Anguish generous bosoms rend; –
Whilst patriot souls their country's fate lament;
Whilst mad with rage demoniac, foul intent,   5
  Embattled legions Despots vainly send
To arrest the immortal mind's expanding ray
  Of everlasting Truth; – I other climes
Where dawns, with hope serene, a brighter day
  Than e'er saw Albion in her happiest times,   10
With mental eye exulting now explore,
  And soon with kindred minds shall haste to enjoy
(Free from the ills which here our peace destroy)
Content and Bliss on Transatlantic shore.

Pantisocracy

No more my Visionary Soul shall dwell
On Joys that were! No more endure to weigh
The Shame and Anguish of the evil Day,
Wisely forgetful! O'er the Ocean swell
Sublime of hope I seek the cottag'd Dell,   5
Where Virtue calm with careless step may stray,
And dancing to the moonlight Roundelay
The Wizard Passions weave an holy Spell.
Eyes that have ach'd with Sorrow! Ye shall weep
Tears of doubt-mingled Joy, like their's who start   10
From Precipices of distemper'd Sleep,
On which the fierce-eyed Fiends their Revels keep,
And see the rising Sun, & feel it dart
New Rays of Pleasance trembling to the Heart.

To the Rev. W. L. Bowles[1]

My heart has thank'd thee, BOWLES! for those soft strains
Whose sadness soothes me, like the murmuring
Of wild-bees in the sunny showers of spring!
For hence not callous to the mourner's pains
Thro' Youth's gay prime and thornless paths I went: 5
And when the *darker* day of life began,
And I did roam, a thought-bewilder'd man!
Their mild and manliest melancholy lent
A mingled charm, such as the pang consign'd
To slumber, tho' the big tear it renew'd;   10
Bidding a strange mysterious PLEASURE brood
Over the wavy and tumultuous mind,
As the great SPIRIT erst with plastic sweep
Mov'd on the darkness of the unform'd deep.

Lines

Composed while climbing the left ascent of Brockley Coomb, in the county of Somerset, May, 1795

With many a pause and oft reverted eye
I climb the Coomb's ascent: sweet songsters near
Warble in shade their wild-wood melody:
Far off th' unvarying Cuckoo soothes my ear.
Up scour the startling stragglers of the Flock   5
That on green plots o'er precipices brouze:
From the forc'd fissures of the naked rock
The Yew tree bursts! Beneath its dark green boughs
(Mid which the May-thorn blends its blossoms white)
Where broad smooth stones jut out in mossy seats,   10

[1] This and the next two poems are printed as they first appeared in 1796.

I rest. – And now have gain'd the topmost site.
Ah! what a luxury of landscape meets
My gaze! Proud Towers, and Cots more dear to me,
Elm-shadow'd Fields, and prospect-bounding Sea!
Deep sighs my lonely heart: I drop the tear: 15
Enchanting spot! O were my SARA here!

The Eolian Harp

Composed 20 August 1795 at Clevedon, Somersetshire

My pensive SARA! thy soft cheek reclin'd
Thus on mine arm, most soothing sweet it is
To sit beside our cot, our cot o'er grown
With white-flower'd Jasmin, and the broad-leav'd Myrtle,
(Meet emblems they of Innocence and Love!)   5
And watch the clouds, that late were rich with light,
Slow sad'ning round, and mark the star of eve
Serenely brilliant (such should Wisdom be)
Shine opposite! How exquisite the scents
Snatch'd from yon bean-field! and the world so hush'd!   10
The stilly murmur of the distant Sea
Tells us of Silence. And that simplest Lute,
Plac'd length-ways in the clasping casement, hark!
How by the desultory breeze caress'd,
Like some coy Maid half-yielding to her Lover,   15
It pours such sweet upbraidings, as must needs
Tempt to repeat the wrong! And now its strings
Boldlier swept, the long sequacious notes
Over delicious surges sink and rise,
Such a soft floating witchery of sound   20
As twilight Elfins make, when they at eve
Voyage on gentle gales from Faery Land,
Where *Melodies* round honey-dropping flowers,

Footless and wild, like birds of Paradise,
Nor pause, nor perch, hovering on untam'd wing   25
[O! the one Life within us and abroad,
Which meets all motion and becomes its soul,
A light in sound, a sound-like power in light,
Rhythm in all thought, and joyance every where —
Methinks, it should have been impossible   30
Not to love all things in a world so fill'd;
Where the breeze warbles, and the mute still air
Is Music slumbering on her instrument.]¹
And thus, my Love! as on the midway slope
Of yonder hill I stretch my limbs at noon,   35
Whilst thro' my half-clos'd eyelids I behold
The sunbeams dance, like diamonds, on the main,
And tranquil muse upon tranquillity;
Full many a thought uncall'd and undetain'd,
And many idle flitting phantasies,   40
Traverse my indolent and passive brain
As wild and various, as the random gales
That swell or flutter on this subject Lute!
And what if all of animated nature
Be but organic Harps diversly fram'd,   45
That tremble into thought, as o'er them sweeps
Plastic and vast, one intellectual Breeze,
At once the Soul of each, and God of all?
But thy more serious eye a mild reproof
Darts, O beloved Woman! nor such thoughts   50
Dim and unhallow'd dost thou now reject,
And biddest me walk humbly with my God.

Meek Daughter in the Family of Christ,
Well hast thou said and holily disprais'd
These shapings of the unregenerate mind,   55
Bubbles that glitter as they rise and break
On vain Philosophy's aye-babbling spring.
For never guiltless may I speak of Him,
Th' INCOMPREHENSIBLE! save when with awe

¹ These eight lines were first published in 1817.

I praise him, and with Faith that inly[1] *feels*; 60
Who with his saving mercies healéd me,
A sinful and most miserable man,
Wilder'd and dark, and gave me to possess
PEACE, and this COT, and THEE, heart-honor'd Maid!

Reflections on Having Left a Place of Retirement

Sermoni propriora. – HOR.[2]

Low was our pretty Cot: our tallest Rose
Peep'd at the chamber-window. We could hear
At silent noon, and eve, and early morn,
The Sea's faint murmur. In the open air
Our Myrtles blossom'd; and across the porch 5
Thick Jasmins twined: the little landscape round
Was green and woody, and refresh'd the eye.
It was a spot which you might aptly call
The Valley of Seclusion! Once I saw
(Hallowing his Sabbath-day by quietness) 10
A wealthy son of Commerce saunter by,
Bristowa's[3] citizen: methought, it calm'd

[1] L'Athée n'est point à mes yeux un faux esprit; je puis vivre avec lui aussi bien et mieux qu'avec le dévot, car il raisonne davantage, mais il lui manque un sens, et mon âme ne se fond point entièrement avec la sienne: il est froid au spectacle le plus ravissant, et il cherche un syllogisme lorsque je rends une action de grâce. – 'Appel à l'impartiale postérité, par la Citoyenne Roland', troisième partie, p. 67 [S.T.C.]. ['In my eyes the atheist is not in the least a false person; I can live with him, as well as, and better than the devout, for he reasons further; but he lacks a certain sense and my mind does not blend entirely with his: he is cold to the most ravishing spectacle and he looks for a syllogism when I return a thanksgiving.']

[2] 'More suitable for prose (or conversation).' Horace's original (Sat.1.4.42) has 'propriora': 'nearer' to prose.

[3] 'Bristol's'. These gently satirical lines recall Satan's visit to Eden in *Paradise Lost* ix, 445–66, where the sight of Paradise makes him 'Stupidly good'.

His thirst of idle gold, and made him muse
With wiser feelings: for he paus'd, and look'd
With a pleas'd sadness, and gaz'd all around,   15
Then eyed our Cottage, and gaz'd round again,
And sigh'd, and said, it was a Blesséd Place.
And we *were* bless'd. Oft with patient ear
Long-listening to the viewless sky-lark's note
(Viewless, or haply for a moment seen   20
Gleaming on sunny wings) in whisper'd tones
I've said to my Belovéd, 'Such, sweet Girl!
The inobtrusive song of Happiness,
Unearthly minstrelsy! then only heard
When the Soul seeks to hear; when all is hush'd,   25
And the Heart listens!'

                    But the time, when first
From that low Dell, steep up the stony Mount
I climb'd with perilous toil and reach'd the top,
Oh! what a goodly scene! *Here* the bleak mount,
The bare bleak mountains speckled thin with sheep;   30
Grey clouds, that shadowing spot the sunny fields;
And river, now with bushy rocks o'er-brow'd,
Now winding bright and full, with naked banks;
And seats, and lawns, and Abbey and the wood,
And cots, and hamlets, and faint city-spire;   35
The Channel *there*, the Islands and white sails,
Dim coasts and cloud-like hills, and shoreless Ocean –
It seem'd like Omnipresence! God, methought,
Had built him there a Temple: the whole World
Seem'd *imag'd* in its vast circumference: 40
No *wish* profan'd my overwhelméd heart.
Blest hour! It was a luxury, – to be!

Ah! quiet Dell! dear Cot, and Mount sublime!
I was constrain'd to quit you. Was it right,
While my unnumber'd breathren toil'd and bled,   45
That I should dream away the entrusted hours
On rose-leaf beds, pampering the coward heart
With feelings all too delicate for use?

Sweet is the tear that from some Howard's[1] eye
Drops on the cheek of one he lifts from earth: 50
And he that works me good with unmov'd face,
Does it but half: he chills me while he aids,
My benefactor, not my brother man!
Yet even this, this cold beneficence
Praise, praise it, O my Soul! oft as thou scann'st   55
The sluggard Pity's vision-weaving tribe!
Who sigh for Wretchedness, yet shun the Wretched,
Nursing in some delicious solitude
Their slothful loves and dainty sympathies!
I therefore go, and join head, heart, and hand,   60
Active and firm, to fight the bloodless fight
Of Science, Freedom, and the Truth in Christ.

 Yet oft when after honourable toil
Rests the tir'd mind, and waking loves to dream,
My spirit shall revisit thee, dear Cot!   65
Thy Jasmin and thy window-peeping Rose,
And Myrtles fearless of the mild sea-air.
And I shall sigh fond wishes – sweet Abode!
Ah! – had none greater! And that all had such!
It might be so – but the time is not yet.   70
Speed it, O Father! Let thy Kingdom come!

This Lime-Tree Bower my Prison

[Addressed to Charles Lamb, of the India House, London]

In the June of 1797 some long-expected friends paid a visit to the author's cottage; and on the morning of their arrival, he met with an accident, which disabled him from walking during the whole time of their stay. One evening, when they had left him for a few hours, he composed the following lines in the garden-bower.

[1] John Howard (1726–90) was a notable prison reformer.

Well, they are gone, and here must I remain,
This lime-tree bower my prison! I have lost
Beauties and feelings, such as would have been
Most sweet to my remembrance even when age
Had dimm'd mine eyes to blindness! They, meanwhile,   5
Friends, whom I never more may meet again,
On springy heath, along the hill-top edge,
Wander in gladness, and wind down, perchance,
To that still roaring dell, of which I told;
The roaring dell, o'erwooded, narrow, deep,   10
And only speckled by the mid-day sun;
Where its slim trunk the ash from rock to rock
Flings arching like a bridge; – that branchless ash,
Unsunn'd and damp, whose few poor yellow leaves
Ne'er tremble in the gale, yet tremble still,   15
Fann'd by the water-fall! and there my friends
Behold the dark green file of long lank weeds,[1]
That all at once (a most fantastic sight!)
Still nod and drip beneath the dripping edge
Of the blue clay-stone.

                Now, my friends emerge   20
Beneath the wide wide Heaven – and view again
The many-steepled tract magnificent
Of hilly fields and meadows, and the sea,
With some fair bark, perhaps, whose sails light up
The slip of smooth clear blue betwixt two Isles   25
Of purple shadow! Yes! they wander on
In gladness all; but thou, methinks, most glad,
My gentle-hearted Charles! for thou hast pined
And hunger'd after Nature, many a year,
In the great City pent, winning thy way   30
With sad yet patient soul, through evil and pain
And strange calamity! Ah! slowly sink
Behind the western ridge, thou glorious Sun!
Shine in the slant beams of the sinking orb,
Ye purple heath-flowers! richlier burn, ye clouds!   35

---

[1] The *Asplenium Scolopendrium*, called in some countries the Adder's Tongue, in others the Hart's Tongue: but Withering gives the Adder's Tongue as the trivial name of the *Ophioglossum* only. [S.T.C.]

Live in the yellow light, ye distant groves!
And kindle, thou blue Ocean! So my friend
Struck with deep joy may stand, as I have stood,
Silent with swimming sense; yea, gazing round
On the wide landscape, gaze till all doth seem   40
Less gross than bodily; and of such hues
As veil the Almighty Spirit, when yet he makes
Spirits perceive his presence.

                    A delight
Comes sudden on my heart, and I am glad
As I myself were there! Nor in this bower,   45
This little lime-tree bower, have I not mark'd
Much that has sooth'd me. Pale beneath the blaze
Hung the transparent foliage; and I watch'd
Some broad and sunny leaf, and lov'd to see
The shadow of the leaf and stem above   50
Dappling its sunshine! And that walnut-tree
Was richly ting'd, and a deep radiance lay
Full on the ancient ivy, which usurps
Those fronting elms, and now, with blackest mass
Makes their dark branches gleam a lighter hue   55
Through the late twilight: and though now the bat
Wheels silent by, and not a swallow twitters,
Yet still the solitary humble-bee
Sings in the bean-flower! Henceforth I shall know
That Nature ne'er deserts the wise and pure;   60
No plot so narrow, be but Nature there,
No waste so vacant, but may well employ
Each faculty of sense, and keep the heart
Awake to Love and Beauty! and sometimes
'Tis well to be bereft of promis'd good,   65
That we may lift the soul, and contemplate
With lively joy the joys we cannot share.
My gentle-hearted Charles! when the last rook
Beat its straight path along the dusky air
Homewards, I blest it! deeming its black wing   70
(Now a dim speck, now vanishing in light)
Had cross'd the mighty Orb's dilated glory,
While thou stood'st gazing; or, when all was still,

Flew creeking o'er thy head, and had a charm
For thee, my gentle-hearted Charles, to whom
No sound is dissonant which tells of Life.

Sonnets Attempted in the Manner of Contemporary Writers[1]

[Signed: 'Nehemiah Higginbottom']

I

Pensive at eve on the *hard* world I mus'd,
And *my poor* heart was sad: so at the Moon
I gaz'd – and sigh'd, and sigh'd! – for, ah! how soon
Eve darkens into night. Mine eye perus'd
With tearful vacancy the *dampy* grass   5
Which wept and glitter'd in the *paly* ray;
And *I did pause me* on my lonely way,
And *mused me* on those *wretched ones* who pass
O'er the black heath of Sorrow. But, alas!
Most of *Myself* I thought: when it befell   10
That the *sooth* Spirit of the breezy wood
Breath'd in mine ear – 'All this is very well;
But much of *one* thing is for *no* thing good.'
Ah! my *poor heart's* INEXPLICABLE SWELL!

[1] 'I sent [to the *Monthly Magazine*] three mock sonnets in ridicule of my own, &
Charles Lloyd's, & Lamb's, &c., &c., – in ridicule of that affectation of
unaffectedness, of jumping & misplaced accent on commonplace epithets, flat lines
forced into poetry by italics (signifying how well & *mouthishly* the Author would
read them), puny pathos, &c, &c. – the instances are almost all taken from mine &
Lloyd's poems – I signed them Nehemiah Higginbottom. I think they may do good
to our young Bards.' [S.T.C., Letter, 1797.] I contributed three sonnets, the first of
which had for its object to excite a good-natured laugh at the spirit of doleful
egotism and at the recurrence of favourite phrases, with the double defect of being
at once trite and licentious. The second, on low, creeping language and thoughts,
under the pretence of *simplicity*. And the third, the phrases of which were
borrowed entirely from my own poems, on the indiscriminate use of elaborate and
swelling language and imagery. [S.T.C. *Biographia Literaria*, ch. i]

II

TO SIMPLICITY

O! I do love thee, meek *Simplicity*!
For of thy lays the lulling simpleness
Goes to my heart and soothes each small distress,
Distress though small, yet haply great to me!
'Tis true on Lady Fortune's gentlest pad   5
I amble on; yet, though I know not why,
So sad I am! – but should a friend and I
Grow cool and *miff*, O! I am *very* sad!
And then with sonnets and with sympathy
My dreamy bosom's mystic woes I pall;   10
Now of my false friend plaining plaintively,
Now raving at mankind in general;
But, whether sad or fierce, 'tis simple all,
All very simple, meek Simplicity!

III

ON A RUINED HOUSE IN A ROMANTIC COUNTRY

And this reft house is that the which he built,
Lamented Jack! And here his malt he pil'd,
Cautious in vain! These rats that squeak so wild,
Squeak, not unconscious of their father's guilt.
Did ye not see her gleaming thro' the glade?   5
Belike, 'twas she, the maiden all forlorn.
What though she milk no cow with crumpled horn,
Yet *aye* she haunts the dale where *erst* she stray'd;
And *aye* beside her stalks her amorous knight!
Still on his thighs their wonted brogues are worn,   10
And thro' those brogues, still tatter'd and betorn,
His hindward charms gleam an unearthly white;
As when thro' broken clouds at night's high noon
Peeps in fair fragments forth the full-orb'd harvest-moon!

Frost at Midnight

The Frost performs its secret ministry,
Unhelped by any wind. The owlet's cry
Came loud – and hark, again! loud as before.
The inmates of my cottage, all at rest,
Have left me to that solitude, which suits   5
Abstruser musings: save that at my side
My cradled infant slumbers peacefully.
'Tis calm indeed! so calm, that it disturbs
And vexes meditation with its strange
And extreme silentness. Sea, hill, and wood,   10
With all the numberless goings-on of life,
Inaudible as dreams! the thin blue flame
Lies on my low-burnt fire, and quivers not;
Only that film,[1] which fluttered on the grate,   15
Still flutters there, the sole unquiet thing.
Methinks, its motion in this hush of nature
Gives it dim sympathies with me who live,
Making it a companionable form,
Whose puny flaps and freaks the idling Spirit   20
By its own moods interprets, every where
Echo or mirror seeking of itself,
And makes a toy of Thought.
                              But O! how oft,
How oft, at school, with most believing mind,
Presageful, have I gazed upon the bars,   25
To watch that fluttering *stranger*! and as oft
With unclosed lids, already had I dreamt
Of my sweet birth-place, and the old church-tower,
Whose bells, the poor man's only music, rang
From morn to evening, all the hot Fair-day,   30
So sweetly, that they stirred and haunted me
With a wild pleasure, falling on mine ear
Most like articulate sounds of things to come!
So gazed I, till the soothing things, I dreamt,

---

[1] In all parts of the kingdom these films are called *strangers* and supposed to
portend the arrival of some absent friend. [S.T.C.] The passage echoes a similar one
in Cowper's *The Task*, iv, 286–98.

Lulled me to sleep, and sleep prolonged my dreams!   35
And so I brooded all the following morn,
Awed by the stern preceptor's face, mine eye
Fixed with mock study on my swimming book:
Save if the door half opened, and I snatched
A hasty glance, and still my heart leaped up,   40
For still I hoped to see the *stranger's* face,
Townsman, or aunt, or sister more beloved,
My play-mate when we both were clothed alike!

   Dear Babe, that sleepest cradled by my side,
Whose gentle breathings, heard in this deep calm,   45
Fill up the interspersèd vacancies
And momentary pauses of the thought!
My babe so beautiful! it thrills my heart
With tender gladness, thus to look at thee,
And think that thou shalt learn far other lore,   50
And in far other scenes! For I was reared
In the great city, pent 'mid cloisters dim,
And saw nought lovely but the sky and stars.
But *thou*, my babe! shalt wander like a breeze
By lakes and sandy shores, beneath the crags   55
Of ancient mountain, and beneath the clouds,
Which image in their bulk both lakes and shores
And mountain crags: so shalt thou see and hear
The lovely shapes and sounds intelligible
Of that eternal language, which thy God   60
Utters, who from eternity doth teach
Himself in all, and all things in himself.
Great universal Teacher! he shall mould
Thy spirit, and by giving make it ask.

   Therefore all seasons shall be sweet to thee,   65
Whether the summer clothe the general earth
With greenness, or the redbreast sit and sing
Betwixt the tufts of snow on the bare branch
Of mossy apple-tree,while the nigh thatch
Smokes in the sun-thaw; whether the eave-drops fall   70
Heard only in the trances of the blast,
Or if the secret ministry of frost

Shall hang them up in silent icicles,
Quietly shining to the quiet Moon.[1]
[February 1798]

Lewti[2]

Or The Circassian Love-Chaunt

At midnight by the stream I roved,
To forget the form I loved,
Image of Lewti! from my mind
Depart; for Lewti is not kind.

The Moon was high, the moonlight gleam   5
    And the shadow of a star
Heaved upon Tamaha's stream;
    But the rock shone brighter far,
The rock half sheltered from my view
By pendent boughs of tressy yew. –   10
So shines my Lewti's forehead fair,
Gleaming through her sable hair.
Image of Lewti! from my mind
Depart; for Lewti is not kind.

[1] When the poem was first published it ended:

Quietly shining to the quiet moon,
Like those, my babe! which ere tomorrow's warmth
Have capp'd their sharp keen points with pendulous drops,
Will catch thine eye, and with their novelty
Suspend thy little soul; then make thee shout,
And stretch and flutter from thy mother's arms
As thou wouldst fly for very eagerness.

In 1808–9 Coleridge removed the last 6 lines, contending in a marginal
annotation that they destroyed the 'rondo, and return upon itself of the Poem'.
    [2] Some lines are taken or adapted from Wordsworth's early 'Beauty and
Moonlight'. [Ed.]

I saw a cloud of palest hue,   15
   Onward to the moon it passed;
Still brighter and more bright it grew,
With floating colours not a few,
   Till it reached the moon at last:
Then the cloud was wholly bright,   20
With a rich and amber light!
And so with many a hope I seek,
   And with such joy I find my Lewti;
And even so my pale wan cheek
   Drinks in as deep a flush of beauty!   25
Nay, treacherous image! leave my mind,
If Lewti never will be kind.

The little cloud – it floats away,
   Away it goes; away so soon?
Alas! it has no power to stay: 30
Its hues are dim, its hues are grey –
   Away it passes from the moon!
How mournfully it seems to fly,
   Ever fading more and more,
To joyless regions of the sky –   35
And now 'tis whiter than before!
As white as my poor cheek will be,
   When, Lewti! on my couch I lie,
A dying man for love of thee.
Nay, treacherous image! leave my mind –   40
And yet, thou didst not look unkind.

   I saw a vapour in the sky,
   Thin, and white, and very high;
I ne'er beheld so thin a cloud:
   Perhaps the breezes that can fly   45
   Now below and now above,
Have snatched aloft the lawny shroud
   Of Lady fair – that died for love.
For maids, as well as youths, have perished
From fruitless love too fondly cherished.   50
Nay, treacherous image! leave my mind –
For Lewti never will be kind.

Hush! my heedless feet from under
   Slip the crumbling banks for ever:
Like echoes to a distant thunder,   55
   They plunge into the gentle river.
The river-swans have heard my tread,
And startle from their reedy bed.
O beauteous birds! methinks ye measure
   Your movements to some heavenly tune!   60
O beauteous birds! 'tis such a pleasure
   To see you move beneath the moon,
I would it were your true delight
To sleep by day and wake all night.

I know the place where Lewti lies,   65
When silent night has closed her eyes:
   It is a breezy jasmine-bower,
The nightingale sings o'er her head:
   Voice of the Night! had I the power
That leafy labyrinth to thread,   70
And creep, like thee, with soundless tread,
I then might view her bosom white
Heaving lovely to my sight,
As these two swans together heave
On the gently swelling wave.   75

Oh! that she saw me in a dream,
   And dreamt that I had died for care;
All pale and wasted I would seem,
   Yet fair withal, as spirits are!
I'd die indeed, if I might see   80
Her bosom heave, and heave for me!
Soothe, gentle image! soothe my mind!
To-morrow Lewti may be kind.

The Nightingale

A Conversation Poem, April 1798

No cloud, no relique of the sunken day
Distinguishes the West, no long thin slip
Of sullen light, no obscure trembling hues.

Come, we will rest on this old mossy bridge!
You see the glimmer of the stream beneath,   5
But hear no murmuring: it flows silently,
O'er its soft bed of verdure. All is still,
A balmy night! and though the stars be dim,
Yet let us think upon the vernal showers
That gladden the green earth, and we shall find   10
A pleasure in the dimness of the stars.
And hark! the Nightingale begins its song,
'Most musical, most melancholy' bird![1]
A melancholy bird? Oh! idle thought!
In Nature there is nothing melancholy.   15
But some night-wandering man whose heart was pierced
With the remembrance of a grievous wrong,
Or slow distemper, or neglected love,
(And so, poor wretch! filled all things with himself,
And made all gentle sounds tell back the tale   20
Of his own sorrow) he, and such as he,
First named these notes a melancholy strain.
And many a poet echoes the conceit;
Poet who hath been building up the rhyme
When he had better far have stretched his limbs   25
Beside a brook in mossy forest-dell,
By sun or moon-light, to the influxes

[1] '*Most musical, most melancholy.*' This passage in Milton possesses an excellence far superior to that of mere description; it is spoken in the character of the melancholy Man, and has therefore a *dramatic* propriety. The Author makes this remark, to rescue himself from the charge of having alluded with levity to a line in Milton; a charge than which none could be more painful to him, except perhaps that of having ridiculed his Bible. [S.T.C.]

Of shapes and sounds and shifting elements
Surrendering his whole spirit, of his song
And of his fame forgetful! so his fame   30
Should share in Nature's immortality,
A venerable thing! and so his song
Should make all Nature lovelier, and itself
Be loved like Nature! But 'twill not be so;
And youths and maidens most poetical,   35
Who lose the deepening twilights of the spring
In ball-rooms and hot theatres, they still
Full of meek sympathy must heave their sighs
O'er Philomela's pity-pleading strains.

My Friend, and thou, our Sister! we have learnt   40
A different lore: we may not thus profane
Nature's sweet voices, always full of love
And joyance! 'Tis the merry Nightingale
That crowds, and hurries, and precipitates
With fast thick warble his delicious notes,   45
As he were fearful that an April night
Would be too short for him to utter forth
His love-chant, and disburthen his full soul
Of all its music!

              And I know a grove
Of large extent, hard by a castle huge,   50
Which the great lord inhabits not; and so
This grove is wild with tangling underwood,
And the trim walks are broken up, and grass,
Thin grass and king-cups grow within the paths.
But never elsewhere in one place I knew   55
So many nightingales; and far and near,
In wood and thicket, over the wide grove,
They answer and provoke each other's song,
With skirmish and capricious passagings,
And murmurs musical and swift jug jug,   60
And one low piping sound more sweet than all –
Stirring the air with such a harmony,
That should you close your eyes, you might almost
Forget it was not day! On moonlight bushes,

Whose dewy leaflets are but half-disclosed,   65
You may perchance behold them on the twigs,
Their bright, bright eyes, their eyes both bright and full,
Glistening, while many a glow-worm in the shade
Lights up her love-torch.

                    A most gentle Maid,
Who dwelleth in her hospital home   70
Hard by the castle, and at latest eve
(Even like a Lady vowed and dedicate
To something more than Nature in the grove)
Glides through the pathways; she knows all their notes,
That gentle Maid! and oft, a moment's space,   75
What time the moon was lost behind a cloud,
Hath heard a pause of silence; till the moon
Emerging, hath awakened earth and sky
With one sensation, and those wakeful birds
Have all burst forth in choral minstrelsy,   80
As if some sudden gale had swept at once
A hundred airy harps! And she hath watched
Many a nightingale perch giddily
On blossomy twig still swinging from the breeze,
And to that motion tune his wanton song   85
Like tipsy joy that reels with tossing head.

  Farewell, O Warbler! till tomorrow eve,
And you, my friends! farewell, a short farewell!
We have been loitering long and pleasantly,
And now for our dear homes. – That strain again!   90
Full fain it would delay me! My dear babe,
Who, capable of no articulate sound,
Mars all things with his imitative lisp,
How he would place his hand beside his ear,
His little hand, the small forefinger up,   95
And bid us listen! And I deem it wise
To make him Nature's play-mate. He knows well
The evening-star; and once, when he awoke
In most distressful mood (some inward pain
Had made up that strange thing, an infant's dream –)   100
I hurried with him to our orchard-plot,

And he beheld the moon, and, hushed at once,
Suspends his sobs, and laughs most silently,
While his fair eyes, that swam with undropped tears,   105
Did glitter in the yellow moon-beam! Well! –
It is a father's tale: But if that Heaven
Should give me life, his childhood shall grow up
Familiar with these songs, that with the night
He may associate joy. – Once more, farewell,
Sweet Nightingale! once more, my friends! farewell.   110

The Ballad of the Dark Ladié

A Fragment

Beneath yon birch with silver bark,
And boughs so pendulous and fair,
The brook falls scatter'd down the rock:
      And all is mossy there!

And there upon the moss she sits,   5
The Dark Ladié in silent pain;
The heavy tear is in her eye,
      And drops and swells again.

Three times she sends her little page
Up the castled mountain's breast,   10
If he might find the knight that wears
      The Griffin for his crest.

The sun was sloping down the sky,
And she had linger'd there all day,
Counting moments, dreaming fears –   15
      Oh wherefore can he stay?

She hears a rustling o'er the brook,
She sees far off a swinging bough!

"'Tis He! 'Tis my betrothéd Knight!
    Lord Falkland, it is Thou!'   20

She springs, she clasps him round the neck,
She sobs a thousand hopes and fears,
Her kisses glowing on his cheeks
    She quenches with her tears.

          *   *   *

'My friends with rude ungentle words   25
They scoff and bid me fly to thee!
O give me shelter in thy breast!
    O shield and shelter me!

'My Henry, I have given thee much,
I gave what I can ne'er recall,   30
I gave my heart, I gave my peace,
    O Heaven! I gave thee all.'

The Knight made answer to the Maid,
While to his heart he held her hand,
'Nine castles hath my noble sire,   35
    None statelier in the land.

'The fairest one shall be my love's,
The fairest castle of the nine!
Wait only till the stars peep out,
    The fairest shall be thine: 40

'Wait only till the hand of eve
Hath wholly closed yon western bars,
And through the dark we two will steal
    Beneath the twinkling stars!' –

'The dark? the dark? No! not the dark?   45
The twinkling stars? How, Henry? How?'
O God! 'twas in the eye of noon
    He pledged his sacred vow!

And in the eye of noon my love
Shall lead me from my mother's door,   50
Sweet boys and girls all clothed in white
    Strewing flowers before:

But first the nodding minstrels go
With music meet for lordly bowers,
The children next in snow-white vests,   55
    Strewing buds and flowers!

And then my love and I shall pace,
My jet black hair in pearly braids,
Between our comely bachelors
    And blushing bridal maids.   60

*   *   *

Kubla Khan

Or, A Vision in a Dream

A FRAGMENT

The following fragment is here published at the request of a
poet of great and deserved celebrity [Lord Byron], and, as far
as the Author's own opinions are concerned, rather as a
psychological curiosity, than on the ground of any supposed
poetic merits.   5

In the summer of the year 1797, the Author, then in ill
health, had retired to a lonely farm-house between Porlock
and Linton, on the Exmoor confines of Somerset and
Devonshire. In consequence of a slight indisposition, an
anodyne had been prescribed, from the effects of which he fell 10
asleep in his chair at the moment that he was reading the
following sentence, or words of the same substance, in
'Purchas's Pilgrimage': 'Here the Khan Kubla commanded a
palace to be built, and a stately garden thereunto. And thus

ten miles of fertile ground were inclosed with a wall.'[1] The   15
Author continued for about three hours in a profound sleep,
at least of the external senses, during which time he has the
most vivid confidence, that he could not have composed less
than from two to three hundred lines; if that indeed can be
called composition in which all the images rose up before him   20
as *things*, with a parallel production of the correspondent
expressions, without any sensation or consciousness of effort.
On awakening he appeared to himself to have a distinct
recollection of the whole, and taking his pen, ink, and paper,
instantly and eagerly wrote down the lines that are here   25
preserved. At this moment he was unfortunately called out by
a person on business from Porlock, and detained by him
above an hour, and on his return to his room found, to his no
small surprise and mortification, that though he still retained
some vague and dim recollection of the general purport of the   30
vision, yet, with the exception of some eight or ten scattered
lines and images, all the rest had passed away like the images
on the surface of a stream into which a stone has been cast,
but, alas! without the after restoration of the latter!

          Then all the charm
Is broken – all that phantom-world so fair
Vanishes, and a thousand circlets spread,
And each mis-shape[s] the other. Stay awhile,
Poor youth! who scarcely dar'st lift up thine eyes –
The stream will soon renew its smoothness, soon
The visions will return! And lo, he stays,
And soon the fragments dim of lovely forms
Come trembling back, unite, and now once more
The pool becomes a mirror.[2]

Yet from the still surviving recollections in his mind, the Author
has frequently purposed to finish for himself what had been

---

[1] 'In Xamdu did Cublai Can build a stately Palace, encompassing sixteene miles
of plaine ground with a wall, wherein are fertile Meddowes, pleasant Springs,
delightfull Streames, and all sorts of beasts of chase and game, and in the middest
thereof a sumptuous house of pleasure.' – *Purchas his Pilgrimage*: Lond. fol. 1626,
Bk. IV, chap. xiii, p. 418.
[2] From Coleridge's 'The Picture; or, the Lover's Resolution', ll. 91–100.

originally, as it were, given to him. Σαμερον αδιον ασω[1]: but the
to-morrow is yet to come.

As a contrast to this vision, I have annexed a fragment of a very
different character, describing with equal fidelity the dream of pain
and disease.[2]

In Xanadu did Kubla Khan
A stately pleasure-dome decree:
Where Alph, the sacred river, ran
Through caverns measureless to man
   Down to a sunless sea.   5
So twice five miles of fertile ground
With walls and towers were girdled round:
And here were gardens bright with sinuous rills,
Where blossomed many an incense-bearing tree;
And here were forests ancient as the hills,   10
Enfolding sunny spots of greenery.

But oh! that deep romantic chasm which slanted
Down the green hill athwart a cedarn cover!
A savage place! as holy and enchanted
As e'er beneath a waning moon was haunted   15
By woman wailing for her demon-lover!
And from the chasm, with ceaseless turmoil seething,
As if this earth in fast thick pants were breathing,
A mighty fountain momently was forced:
Amid whose swift half-intermitted burst   20
Huge fragments vaulted like rebounding hail,
Or chaffy grain beneath the thresher's flail:
And 'mid these dancing rocks at once and ever
It flung up momently the sacred river.
Five miles meandering with a mazy motion   25
Through wood and dale the sacred river ran,
Then reached the caverns measureless to man,
And sank in tumult to a lifeless ocean:
And 'mid this tumult Kubla heard from far
Ancestral voices prophesying war!   30

[1] 'Tomorrow I shall sing more sweetly'. After Theocritus i. 145. [E.H.C.]
[2] See 'The Pains of Sleep', p. 93.

The shadow of the dome of pleasure
Floated midway on the waves;
Where was heard the mingled measure
From the fountain and the caves.
It was a miracle of rare device,   35
A sunny pleasure-dome with caves of ice!

A damsel with a dulcimer
In a vision once I saw:
It was an Abyssinian maid,
And on her dulcimer she played,   40
Singing of Mount Abora.
Could I revive within me
Her symphony and song,
To such a deep delight 'twould win me,
That with music loud and long,   45
I would build that dome in air,
That sunny dome! those caves of ice!
And all who heard should see them there,
And all should cry, Beware! Beware!
His flashing eyes, his floating hair!   50
Weave a circle round him thrice,
And close your eyes with holy dread,
For he on honey-dew hath fed,
And drunk the milk of Paradise.

The Rime of the Ancient Mariner[1]

IN SEVEN PARTS

Facile credo, plures esse Naturas invisibiles quam visibles in rerum
universitate. Sed horum omnium familiam quis nobis enarrabit? et
gradus et cognationes et discrimina et singulorum munera? Quid
agunt? quae loca habitant? Harum rerum notitiam semper ambivit
ingenium humanum, nunquam attigit. Juvat, interea, non diffiteor,

[1] First published in 1798; the present version was current from 1817 onwards.

quandoque in animo, tanquam in Tabulâ, majoris et melioris
mundi imaginem contemplari: ne mens assuefacta hodiernae vitae
minutiis se contrahat nimis, & tota subsidat in pusillas cogitationes.
Sed veritati interea invigilandum est, modusque servandus, ut
certa ab incertis, diem a nocte, distinguamus. – T. BURNET,
Archaeol. Phil. p. 68.[1]

PART THE FIRST

An ancient Mariner
meeteth three
Gallants bidden to a
wedding-feast, and
detaineth one.

It is an ancient Mariner,
And he stoppeth one of three.
'By thy long grey beard and glittering eye,
Now wherefore stopp'st thou me?

The Bridegroom's doors are opened wide,   5
And I am next of kin;
The guests are met, the feast is set;
May'st hear the merry din.'

He holds him with his skinny hand,
'There was a ship,' quoth he.   10
'Hold off! unhand me, greybeard loon!'
Eftsoons his hand dropt he.

The Wedding-Guest
is spellbound by the
eye of the old sea-
faring man, and
constrained to hear
his tale.

He holds him with his glittering eye –
The Wedding-Guest stood still,
And listens like a three years child: 15
The Mariner hath his will.

The Wedding-Guest sat on a stone:
He cannot choose but hear;

---

[1] Tr: I can easily believe, that there are more invisible than visible beings in the
universe . . . But who will explain to us this great family – their ranks, their
relationships, their differences and their respective functions? [What do they do,
and where do they live? – *S.T.C.'s addition*] Human cleverness has always sought
knowledge of these things, never attained it. At the same time I do not deny the
pleasure of sometimes contemplating, as in a picture, the image of a greater and
better world; lest the mind, inured to the details of everyday life, should contract
and sink down into paltry thoughts. But meanwhile we must be vigilant for truth
and observe proportion, so that we can distinguish the certain from the uncertain,
day from night.

And thus spake on that ancient man,
The bright-eyed Mariner.   20

'The ship was cheered, the harbour cleared,
Merrily did we drop
Below the kirk, below the hill,
Below the lighthouse top.

The Mariner tells how the ship sailed southward with a good wind and fair weather, till it reached the Line.

The Sun came up upon the left,   25
Out of the sea came he!
And he shone bright, and on the right
Went down into the sea.

Higher and higher every day,
Till over the mast at noon –'   30
The Wedding-Guest here beat his breast,
For he heard the loud bassoon.

The Wedding-Guest heareth the bridal music; but the Mariner continueth his tale.

The bride hath paced into the hall,
Red as a rose is she;
Nodding their heads before her goes   35
The merry minstrelsy.

The Wedding-Guest he beat his breast,
Yet he cannot choose but hear;
And thus spake on that ancient man,
The bright-eyed Mariner.   40

The ship driven by a storm toward the south pole

And now the STORM-BLAST came, and he
Was tyrannous and strong:
He struck with his o'ertaking wings,
And chased us south along.

With sloping masts and dipping prow,   45
As who pursued with yell and blow
Still treads the shadow of his foe,
And forward bends his head,
The ship drove fast, loud roared the blast,
And southward aye we fled   50

And now there came both mist and snow,
And it grew wondrous cold:
And ice, mast-high, came floating by,
As green as emerald.

The land of ice, and
of fearful sounds
where no living thing
was to be seen.

And through the drifts the snowy clifts   55
Did send a dismal sheen:
Nor shapes of men nor beasts we ken –
The ice was all between.

The ice was here, the ice was there,
The ice was all around: 60
It cracked and growled, and roared and
    howled,
Like noises in a swound!

Till a great seabird,
called the Albatross,
came through the
snow-fog, and was
received with great
joy and hospitality.

At length did cross an Albatross,
Thorough the fog it came;
As if it had been a Christian soul,   65
We hailed it in God's name.

It ate the food it n'er had eat,
And round and round it flew.
The ice did split with a thunder-fit;
The helmsman steered us through!   70

And lo! the Albatross
proveth a bird of
good omen, and
followeth the ship as
it returned northward
through fog and
floating ice.

And a good south wind sprung up behind;
The Albatross did follow,
And every day, for food or play,
Came to the mariners' hollo!

In mist or cloud, on mast or shroud,   75
It perched for vespers nine;
Whiles all the night, through fog-smoke white,
Glimmered the white Moon-shine.

The ancient Mariner
inhospitably killeth
the pious bird of
good-omen.

'God save thee, ancient Mariner!
From the fiends, that plague thee thus! –   80
Why look'st thou so?' – With my cross-bow
I shot the ALBATROSS.

PART THE SECOND

The Sun now rose upon the right:
Out of the sea came he,
Still hid in mist, and on the left 85
Went down into the sea.

And the good south wind still blew behind,
But no sweet bird did follow,
Nor any day for food or play
Came to the mariners' hollo! 90

His shipmates cry out against the ancient Mariner, for killing the bird of good luck.

And I had done a hellish thing,
And it would work 'em woe:
For all averred, I had killed the bird
That made the breeze to blow.
Ah wretch! said they, the bird to slay 95
That made the breeze to blow!

But when the fog cleared off, they justify the same, and thus make themselves accomplices in the crime.

Nor dim nor red, like God's own head,
The glorious Sun uprist:
Then all averred, I had killed the bird
That brought the fog and mist. 100
'Twas right, said they, such birds to slay,
That bring the fog and mist.

The fair breeze continues: the ship enters the Pacific Ocean, and sails northward, even till it reaches the Line.

The fair breeze blew, the white foam flew,
The furrow followed free;
We were the first that ever burst 105
Into that silent sea.

The ship hath been suddenly becalmed.

Down dropt the breeze, the sails dropt down,
'Twas sad as sad could be;
And we did speak only to break
The silence of the sea! 110

All in a hot and copper sky,
The bloody Sun, at noon,

Right up above the mast did stand,
No bigger than the Moon.

Day after day, day after day,   115
We stuck, nor breath nor motion;
As idle as a painted ship
Upon a painted ocean.

And the Albatross
begins to be
avenged.

Water, water, every where,
And all the boards did shrink;   120
Water, water, every where,
Nor any drop to drink.

The very deep did rot: O Christ!
That ever this should be!
Yea, slimy things did crawl with legs   125
Upon the slimy sea.

About, about, in reel and rout
The death-fires danced at night;
The water, like a witch's oils,
Burnt green, and blue and white.   130

A Spirit had followed
them; one of the
invisible inhabitants
of this planet, neither
departed souls nor
angels; concerning

And some in dreams assuréd were
Of the spirit that plagued us so;
Nine fathom deep he had followed us
From the land of mist and snow.

whom the learned Jew, Josephus, and the Platonic Constantinopolitan, Michael Psellus, may
be consulted. They are very numerous, and there is no climate or element without one or more.

And every tongue, through utter drought,   135
Was withered at the root;
We could not speak, no more than if
We had been choked with soot.

The shipmates, in
their sore distress,
would fain throw the
whole guilt on the
ancient Mariner: in
sign whereof they

Ah! well a-day! what evil looks
Had I from old and young!   140
Instead of the cross, the Albatross
About my neck was hung.

hang the dead sea-bird round his neck.

PART THE THIRD

There passed a weary time. Each throat
Was parched, and glazed each eye.
A weary time! a weary time!   145
How glazed each weary eye,
The ancient Mariner beholdeth a sign in the element afar off.
When looking westward, I beheld
A something in the sky.

At first it seemed a little speck,
And then it seemed a mist;   150
It moved and moved, and took at last
A certain shape, I wist.

A speck, a mist, a shape, I wist!
And still it neared and neared:
As if it dodged a water-sprite,   155
It plunged and tacked and veered.

At its nearer approach, it seemeth to him to be a ship; and at a dear ransom he freeth his speech from the bonds of thirst.
With throats unslaked, with black lips baked,
We could nor laugh nor wail;
Through utter drought all dumb we stood!
I bit my arm, I sucked the blood,   160
And cried, A sail! a sail!

With throats unslaked, with black lips baked,
Agape they heard me call:
A flash of joy;
Gramercy! they for joy did grin,

And all at once their breath drew in,   165
As they were drinking all.

And horror follows. For can it be a ship that comes onward without wind or tide?
See! see! (I cried) she tacks no more!
Hither to work us weal;
Without a breeze, without a tide,
She steadies with upright keel!   170

The western wave was all a-flame.
The day was well nigh done!
Almost upon the western wave
Rested the broad bright Sun;
When that strange shape drove suddenly   175
Betwixt us and the Sun.

And straight the Sun was flecked with bars,
(Heaven's Mother send us grace!)
As if through a dungeon-grate he peered
With broad and burning face.   180

It seemeth him but the skeleton of a ship.

Alas! (thought I, and my heart beat loud)
How fast she nears and nears!
Are those *her* sails that glance in the Sun,
Like restless gossameres?

Are those *her* ribs through which the Sun   185
Did peer, as through a grate?
And is that Woman all her crew?

And its ribs are seen as bars on the face of the setting Sun.

Is that a DEATH? and are there two?
Is DEATH that woman's mate?

The spectre-woman and her death-mate, and no other on board the skeleton ship.

Her lips were red, *her* looks were free,   190
Her locks were yellow as gold:
Her skin was as white as leprosy,
The Night-mare LIFE-IN-DEATH was she,
Who thicks man's blood with cold.

Like vessel, like crew!

The naked hulk alongside came,   195
And the twain were casting dice;
'The game is done! I've won! I've won!'
Quoth she, and whistles thrice.

DEATH and LIFE-IN-DEATH have diced for the ship's crew, and she (the latter) winneth the ancient Mariner.

The Sun's rim dips; the stars rush out:
At one stride comes the dark;   200
With far-heard whisper, o'er the sea,
Off shot the spectre-bark.

No twilight within the courts of the Sun.

We listened and looked sideways up!
Fear at my heart, as at a cup,
My life-blood seemed to sip!   205
The stars were dim, and thick the night,
The steerman's face by his lamp gleamed white;
From the sails the dew did drip –
Till clomb above the eastern bar

At the rising of the Moon,

The hornéd Moon, with one bright star   210
Within the nether tip.

One after another,

One after one, by the star-dogged Moon,

Too quick for groan or sigh,
Each turned his face with a ghastly pang,
And cursed me with his eye.   215

His shipmates drop
down dead.

Four times fifty living men,
(And I heard nor sigh nor groan)
With heavy thump, a lifeless lump,
They dropped down one by one,

But LIFE-IN-DEATH
begins her work on
the Ancient Mariner.

The souls did from their bodies fly, –
They fled to bliss or woe!   220
And every soul, it passed me by,
Like the whizz of my cross-bow!

PART THE FOURTH

The wedding-guest
feareth that a spirit is
talking to him;

'I fear thee, ancient Mariner!
I fear thy skinny hand!   225
And thou art long, and lank, and brown,
As is the ribbed sea-sand.[1]

I fear thee and thy glittering eye,
And thy skinny hand, so brown.' –

But the ancient
Mariner assureth him
of his bodily life, and
proceedeth to relate
his horrible penance.

Fear not, fear not, thou Wedding-Guest!   230
This body dropt not down.

Alone, alone, all, all alone,
Alone on a wide wide sea!
And never a saint took pity on
My soul in agony.   235

He despiseth the
creatures of the calm,

The many men, so beautiful!
And they all dead did lie:

[1] For the last two lines of this stanza, I am indebted to Mr WORDSWORTH. It was on a delightful walk from Nether Stowey to Dulverton, with him and his sister, in the Autumn of 1797, that this Poem was planned, and in part composed. [S.T.C.]

And a thousand thousand slimy things
Lived on; and so did I.

And envieth that *they*
should live, and so
many lie dead.

I looked upon the rotting sea,
And drew my eyes away;   240
I looked upon the rotting deck,
And there the dead men lay.

I looked to Heaven, and tried to pray;
But or ever a prayer had gusht,   245
A wicked whisper came, and made
My heart as dry as dust.

I closed my lids, and kept them close,
And the balls like pulses beat;
For the sky and the sea, and the sea and the
     sky   250
Lay like a load on my weary eye,
And the dead were at my feet.

But the curse liveth
for him in the eye of
the dead men.

The cold sweat melted from their limbs,
Nor rot nor reek did they:
The look with which they looked on me   255
Had never passed away.

An orphan's curse would drag to Hell
A spirit from on high;
But oh! more horrible than that
Is the curse in a dead man's eye!   260
Seven days, seven nights, I saw that curse,
And yet I could not die.

In his loneliness and
fixedness he yearneth
towards the
journeying Moon,
and the stars that still
sojourn, yet still move
onward; and
every where the blue sky belongs to them, and is their appointed rest, and their native country and
their own natural homes, which they enter unannounced, as lords that are certainly expected and yet
there is a silent joy at their arrival.

The moving Moon went up the sky,
And no where did abide:
Softly she was going up,   265
And a star or two beside –

Her beams bemocked the sultry main,
Like April hoar-frost spread;

But where the ship's huge shadow lay,
The charméd water burnt alway   270
A still and awful red.

By the light of the
Moon he beholdeth
God's creatures of
the great calm.

Beyond the shadow of the ship,
I watched the water-snakes:
They moved in tracks of shining white,
And when they reared, the elfish light   275
Fell off in hoary flakes.

Within the shadow of the ship
I watched their rich attire:
Blue, glossy green, and velvet black,
They coiled and swarm; and every track   280
Was a flash of golden fire.

Their beauty and
their happiness.

O happy living things! no tongue
Their beauty might declare:
A spring of love gushed from my heart,

He blesseth them in
his heart.

And I blessed them unaware: 285
Sure my kind saint took pity on me,
And I blessed them unaware.

The spell begins to
break.

The self same moment I could pray;
And from my neck so free
The Albatross fell off, and sank   290
Like lead into the sea.

PART THE FIFTH

O sleep! it is a gentle thing,
Beloved from pole to pole!
To Mary Queen the praise be given!
She sent the gentle sleep from Heaven,   295
That slid into my soul.

By grace of the holy
Mother, the ancient
Mariner is refreshed
with rain.

The silly buckets on the deck,
That had so long remained,
I dreamt that they were filled with dew;
And when I awoke, it rained.   300

My lips were wet, my throat was cold,
My garments all were dank:
Sure I had drunken in my dreams,
And still my body drank.

I moved, and could not feel my limbs: 305
I was so light – almost
I thought that I had died in sleep,
And was a blesséd ghost.

He heareth sounds
and seeth strange
sights and
commotions in the
sky and the element.

And soon I heard a roaring wind:
It did not come anear;   310
But with its sound it shook the sails,
That were so thin and sere.

The upper air burst into life!
And a hundred fire-flags sheen,
To and fro they were hurried about!   315
And to and fro, and in and out,
The wan stars danced between.

And the coming wind did roar more loud,
And the sails did sigh like sedge;
And the rain poured down from one
    black cloud;   320
The Moon was at its edge.

The thick black cloud was cleft, and still
The Moon was at its side:
Like waters shot from some high crag,
The lightning fell with never a jag,   325
A river steep and wide.

The bodies of the
ship's crew are
inspirited, and the
ship moves on;

The loud wind never reached the ship,
Yet now the ship moved on!
Beneath the lightning and the Moon
The dead men gave a groan.   330

They groaned, they stirred, they all uprose,
Nor spake, nor moved their eyes;

It had been strange, even in a dream,
To have seen those dead men rise.

The helmsman steered, the ship moved on;   335
Yet never a breeze up blew;
The mariners all 'gan work the ropes,
Where they were wont to do;
They raised their limbs like lifeless tools –
We were a ghastly crew.   340

The body of my brother's son
Stood by me, knee to knee:
The body and I pulled at one rope,
But he said nought to me.

'I fear thee, ancient Mariner!'   345
Be calm, thou Wedding-Guest!
'Twas not those souls that fled in pain,
Which to their corses came again,
But a troop of spirits blest:

But not by the souls of men, nor by demons of earth or middle air, but by a blessed troop of angelic spirits, sent down by the invocation of the guardian saint.

For when it dawned – they dropped their
          arms,   350
And clustered round the mast;
Sweet sounds rose slowly through their mouths,
And from their bodies passed.

Around, around, flew each sweet sound,
Then darted to the Sun;   355
Slowly the sounds came back again,
Now mixed, now one by one.

Sometimes a-dropping from the sky
I heard the sky-lark sing;
Sometimes all little birds that are,   360
How they seemed to fill the sea and air
With their sweet jargoning!

And now 'twas like all instruments,
Now like a lonely flute;

And now it is an angel's song,   365
That makes the Heavens be mute.

It ceased; yet still the sails made on
A pleasant noise till noon,
A noise like of a hidden brook
In the leafy month of June,   370
That to the sleeping woods all night
Singeth a quiet tune.

Till noon we quietly sailed on,
Yet never a breeze did breathe:
Slowly and smoothly went the ship,   375
Moved onward from beneath.

The lonesome spirit from the south pole carries on the ship as far as the Line, in obedience to the angelic troop, but still requireth vengeance.

Under the keel nine fathom deep,
From the land of mist and snow,
The spirit slid: and it was he
That made the ship to go.   380
The sails at noon left off their tune,
And the ship stood still also.

The Sun, right up above the mast,
Had fixed her to the ocean:
But in a minute she 'gan stir,   385
With a short uneasy motion –
Backwards and forwards half her length
With a short uneasy motion.

Then like a pawing horse let go,
She made a sudden bound: 390
It flung the blood into my head,
And I fell down in a swound.

The Polar Spirit's fellow dæmons, the invisible inhabitants of the element, take part in his wrong; and two of them relate, one to the other, that penance long and

How long in that same fit I lay,
I have not to declare;
But ere my living life returned,   395
I heard and in my soul discerned
TWO VOICES in the air.

heavy for the ancient
Mariner hath been
accorded to the polar
Spirit, who returneth
southward.

'Is it he?' quoth one. 'Is this the man?
By him who died on cross,
With his cruel bow he laid full low 400
The harmless Albatross.

The spirit who bideth by himself
In the land of mist and snow,
He loved the bird that loved the man
Who shot him with his bow.' 405

The other was a softer voice,
As soft as honey-dew:
Quoth he, 'The man hath penance done,
And penance more will do.'

PART THE SIXTH

FIRST VOICE
But tell me, tell me! speak again, 410
Thy soft response renewing –
What makes that ship drive on so fast?
What is the OCEAN doing?

SECOND VOICE
Still as a slave before his lord,
The OCEAN hath no blast; 415
His great bright eye most silently
Up to the Moon is cast –

If he may know which way to go;
For she guides him smooth or grim.
See, brother, see! how graciously 420
She looketh down on him.

FIRST VOICE
The Mariner hath
been cast into a
trance; for the angelic
power causeth the
vessel to drive
northward faster than
human life could
endure.
But why drives on that ship so fast,
Without or wave or wind?

SECOND VOICE
The air is cut away before,
And closes from behind. 425

Fly, brother, fly! more high, more high!
Or we shall be belated:
For slow and slow that ship will go,
When the Mariner's trance is abated.

I woke, and we were sailing on   430
As in a gentle weather:
'Twas night, calm night, the Moon was high;
The dead men stood together.

The super natural motion is retarded; the Mariner awakes, and his penance begins anew.

All stood together on the deck,
For a charnel-dungeon fitter: 435
All fixed on me their stony eyes,
That in the Moon did glitter.

The pang, the curse, with which they died,
Had never passed away:
I could not draw my eyes from theirs,   440
Nor turn them up to pray.

And now this spell was snapt: once more
I viewed the ocean green,
And looked far forth, yet little saw
Of what had else been seen –   445

The curse is finally expiated.

Like one, that on a lonesome road
Doth walk in fear and dread,
And having once turned round walks on,
And turns no more his head;
Because he knows, a frightful fiend   450
Doth close behind him tread.

But soon there breathed a wind on me,
Nor sound nor motion made:
Its path was not upon the sea,
In ripple or in shade.   455

It raised my hair, it fanned my cheek
Like a meadow-gale of spring –

It mingled strangely with my fears,
Yet it felt like a welcoming.

Swiftly, swiftly flew the ship,   460
Yet she sailed softly too:
Sweetly, sweetly blew the breeze –
On me alone it blew.

*And the ancient
Mariner beholdeth
his native country.*

Oh! dream of joy! is this indeed
The light-house top I see?   465
Is this the hill? is this the kirk?
Is this mine own countree?

We drifted o'er the harbour-bar,
And I with sobs did pray –
O let me be awake, my God!   470
Or let me sleep alway.

The harbour-bay was clear as glass,
So smoothly it was strewn!
And on the bay the moonlight lay,
And the shadow of the Moon.   475

The rock shone bright, the kirk no less,
That stands above the rock:
The moonlight steeped in silentness
The steady weathercock.

And the bay was white with silent light,   480

*The angelic spirits
leave the dead
bodies,*

Till rising from the same,
Full many shapes, that shadows were,
In crimson colours came.

*And appear in their
own forms of light.*

A little distance from the prow
Those crimson shadows were: 485
I turned my eyes upon the deck –
Each corse lay flat, lifeless and flat,
And, by the holy rood!
Oh, Christ! what saw I there!

A man all light, a seraph-man, 490
On every corse there stood.

This seraph-band, each waved his hand:
It was a heavenly sight!
They stood as signals to the land,
Each one a lovely light: 495

This seraph-band, each waved his hand,
No voice did they impart –
No voice; but oh! the silence sank
Like music on my heart.

But soon I heard the dash of oars, 500
I heard the Pilot's cheer;
My head was turned perforce away,
And I saw a boat appear.

The Pilot, and the Pilot's boy,
I heard them coming fast: 505
Dear Lord in Heaven! it was a joy
The dead men could not blast.

I saw a third – I heard his voice:
It is the Hermit good!
He singeth loud his godly hymns 510
That he makes in the wood.
He'll shrieve my soul, he'll wash away
The Albatross's blood.

PART THE SEVENTH

The Hermit of the Wood,

This Hermit good lives in that wood
Which slopes down to the sea. 515
How loudly his sweet voice he rears!
He loves to talk with marineres
That come from a far countree.
He kneels at morn, and noon and eve –

He hath a cushion plump: 520
It is the moss that wholly hides
The rotted old oak-stump.

The skiff-boat neared: I heard them talk,
'Why, this is strange, I trow!
Where are those lights so many and fair,   525
That signal made but now?'

Approacheth the ship with wonder.

'Strange, by my faith!' the Hermit said –
'And they answered not our cheer!
The planks looked warped! and see those sails,
How thin they are and sere!   530
I never saw aught like to them,
Unless perchance it were

Brown skeletons of leaves that lag
My forest-brook along;
When the ivy-tod is heavy with snow,   535
And the owlet whoops to the wolf below,
That eats the she-wolf's young.'

'Dear Lord! it hath a fiendish look –
(The Pilot made reply)
I am a-feared' – 'Push on, push on!'
Said the Hermit cheerily.

The boat came closer to the ship,
But I nor spake nor stirred;
The boat came close beneath the ship,
And straight a sound was heard.   545

The ship suddenly sinketh.

Under the water it rumbled on,
Still louder and more dread:
It reached the ship, it split the bay;
The ship went down like lead.

The ancient Mariner is saved in the Pilot's boat.

Stunned by that loud and dreadful sound,
Which sky and ocean smote,   550
Like one that hath been seven days drowned
My body lay afloat;

But swift as dreams, myself I found
Within the Pilot's boat.   555

Upon the whirl, where sank the ship,
The boat spun round and round;
And all was still, save that the hill
Was telling of the sound.

I moved my lips – the Pilot shrieked   560
And fell down in a fit;
The holy Hermit raised his eyes,
And prayed where he did sit.

I took the oars: the Pilot's boy,
Who now doth crazy go,   565
Laughed loud and long, and all the while
His eyes went to and fro.
'Ha! ha!' quoth he, 'full plain I see,
The Devil knows how to row.'

And now, all in my own countree,   570
I stood on the firm land!
The Hermit stepped forth from the boat,
And scarcely he could stand.

The ancient Mariner earnestly entreateth the Hermit to shrieve him; and the penance of life falls on him.

'O shrieve me, shrieve me, holy man!'
The Hermit crossed his brow.   575
'Say quick,' quoth he, 'I bid thee say –
What manner of man art thou?'

Forthwith this frame of mine was wrenched
With a woeful agony,
Which forced me to begin my tale;   580
And then it left me free.

And ever and anon throughout his future life an agony constraineth him to travel from land to land.

Since then, at an uncertain hour,
The agony returns:
And till my ghastly tale is told,
This heart within me burns.   585

I pass, like night, from land to land;
I have strange power of speech;
That moment that his face I see,
I know the man that must hear me:
To him my tale I teach.   590

What loud uproar bursts from that door!
The wedding-guests are there:
But in the garden-bower the bride
And bride-maids singing are:
And hark the little vesper bell,   595
Which biddeth me to prayer!

O Wedding-Guest! this soul hath been
Alone on a wide wide sea:
So lonely 'twas, that God himself
Scarce seeméd there to be.   600

O sweeter than the marriage-feast,
'Tis sweeter far to me,
To walk together to the kirk
With a goodly company! –

To walk together to the kirk,   605
And all together pray,
While each to his great Father bends,
Old men, and babes, and loving friends
And youths and maidens gay!

And to teach, by his own example, love and reverence to all things that God made and loveth.

Farewell, farewell! but this I tell   610
To thee, thou Wedding-Guest!
He prayeth well, who loveth well
Both man and bird and beast.

He prayeth best, who loveth best
All things both great and small;   615
For the dear God who loveth us,
He made and loveth all.'

The Mariner, whose eye is bright,
Whose beard with age is hoar,
Is gone: and now the Wedding-Guest   620
Turned from the bridegroom's door.

He went like one that hath been stunned,
And is of sense forlorn:
A sadder and a wiser man,
He rose the morrow morn.   625

France: An Ode[1]

I

Ye Clouds! that far above me float and pause,
   Whose pathless march no mortal may controul!
   Ye Ocean-Waves! that, wheresoe'er ye roll,
Yield homage only to eternal laws!
Ye Woods! that listen to the night-birds singing,   5
   Midway the smooth and perilous slope reclined,
Save when your own imperious branches swinging,
   Have made a solemn music of the wind!
Where, like a man beloved of God,
Through glooms, which never woodman trod,   10
      How oft, pursuing fancies holy,
My moonlight way o'er flowering weeds I wound,
      Inspired, beyond the guess of folly,
By each rude shape and wild unconquerable sound!
O ye loud Waves! and O ye Forests high!   15
   And O ye Clouds that far above me soared!
Thou rising Sun! thou blue rejoicing Sky!
   Yea, every thing that is and will be free!
   Bear witness for me, wheresoe'er ye be,
   With what deep worship I have still adored   20
      The spirit of divinest Liberty.

[1] In 1795 the Swiss cantons, traditionally free, were suppressed by the French.

II

When France in wrath her giant-limbs upreared,
   And with that oath, which smote air, earth, and sea,
   Stamped her strong foot and said she would be free,
Bear witness for me, how I hoped and feared!   25
With what a joy my lofty gratulation
   Unawed I sang, amid a slavish band:
And when to whelm the disenchanted nation,
   Like fiends embattled by a wizard's wand,
     The Monarchs marched in evil day,   30
     And Britain joined the dire array;
   Though dear her shores and circling ocean,
Though many friendships, many youthful loves
   Had swoln the patriot emotion
And flung a magic light o'er all her hills and groves;   35
Yet still my voice, unaltered, sang defeat
   To all that braved the tyrant-quelling lance,
And shame too long delayed and vain retreat!
For ne'er, O Liberty! with partial aim
I dimmed thy light or damped thy holy flame;   40
   But blessed the paeans of delivered France,
And hung my head and wept at Britain's name.

III

'And what,' I said, 'though Blasphemy's loud scream
   With that sweet music of deliverance strove!
   Though all the fierce and drunken passions wove   45
A dance more wild than e'er was maniac's dream!
   Ye storms, that round the dawning East assembled,
The Sun was rising, though ye hid his light!'
   And when, to soothe my soul, that hoped and trembled,
The dissonance ceased, and all seemed calm and bright;   50
   When France her front deep-scarr'd and gory,
   Concealed with clustering wreaths of glory;
     When, insupportably advancing,
   Her arm made mockery of the warrior's ramp;
     While timid looks of fury glancing,   55
   Domestic treason, crushed beneath her fatal stamp,
Writhed like a wounded dragon in his gore;
   Then I reproached my fears that would not flee;

'And soon,' I said, 'shall Wisdom teach her lore
In the low huts of them that toil and groan!   60
And, conquering by her happiness alone,
     Shall France compel the nations to be free,
Till Love and Joy look round, and call the Earth their own.'

IV

Forgive me, Freedom! O forgive those dreams!
     I hear thy voice, I hear thy loud lament,   65
     From bleak Helvetia's icy caverns sent –
I hear thy groans upon her blood-stained streams!
     Heroes, that for your peaceful country perished,
And ye that, fleeing, spot your mountain-snows
     With bleeding wounds; forgive me, that I cherished   70
One thought that ever blessed your cruel foes!
     To scatter rage, and traitorous guilt,
     Where Peace her jealous home had built;
       A patriot-race to disinherit
Of all that made their stormy wilds so dear;   75
       And with inexpiable spirit
To taint the bloodless freedom of the mountaineer –
O France, that mockest Heaven, adulterous, blind,
     And patriot only in pernicious toils!
Are these thy boasts, Champion of human kind?   80
     To mix with Kings in the low lust of sway,
Yell in the hunt, and share the murderous prey;
To insult the shrine of Liberty with spoils
     From freemen torn; to tempt and to betray?

V

     The Sensual and the Dark rebel in vain,   85
     Slaves by their own compulsion! In mad game
     They burst their manacles and wear the name
       Of Freedom, graven on a heavier chain!
O Liberty! with profitless endeavour
Have I pursued thee, many a weary hour;   90
     But thou nor swell'st the victor's strain, nor ever
Didst breathe thy soul in forms of human power.
     Alike from all, howe'er they praise thee,
     (Nor prayer, nor boastful name delays thee)

Alike from Priestcraft's harpy minions, 95
  And factious Blasphemy's obscener slaves,
    Thou speedest on thy subtle pinions,
The guide of homeless winds, and playmate of the waves!
And there I felt thee! – on that sea-cliff's verge,
  Whose pines, scarce travelled by the breeze above, 100
Had made one murmur with the distant surge!
Yes, while I stood and gazed, my temples bare,
And shot my being through earth, sea, and air,
  Possessing all things with intensest love,
  O Liberty! my spirit felt thee there. 105

Fears in Solitude

Written in April 1798, during the Alarm of an Invasion

A green and silent spot, amid the hills,
A small and silent dell! O'er stiller place
No singing sky-lark ever poised himself.
The hills are heathy, save that swelling slope,
Which hath a gay and gorgeous covering on, 5
All golden with the never-bloomless furze,
Which now blooms most profusely: but the dell,
Bathed by the mist, is fresh and delicate
As vernal corn-field, or the unripe flax,
When, through its half-transparent stalks, at eve, 10
The level sunshine glimmers with green light.
Oh! 'tis a quiet spirit-healing nook!
Which all, methinks, would love; but chiefly he,
The humble man, who, in his youthful years,
Knew just so much of folly, as had made 15
His early manhood more securely wise!
Here he might lie on fern or withered heath,
While from the singing-lark (that sings unseen
The minstrelsy that solitude loves best),
And from the sun, and from the breezy air, 20

Sweet influences trembled o'er his frame;
And he, with many feelings, many thoughts,
Made up a meditative joy, and found
Religious meanings in the forms of Nature!
And so, his senses gradually wrapt   25
In a half sleep, he dreams of better worlds,
And dreaming hears thee still, O singing-lark,
That singest like an angel in the clouds!

  My God! it is a melancholy thing
For such a man, who would full fain preserve   30
His soul in calmness, yet perforce must feel
For all his human brethren – O my God!
It weighs upon the heart, that he must think
What uproar and what strife may now be stirring
This way or that way o'er these silent hills –   35
Invasion, and the thunder and the shout,
And all the crash of onset; fear and rage,
And undetermined conflict – even now,
Even now, perchance, and in his native isle:
Carnage and groans beneath this blessed sun!   40
We have offended, Oh! my countrymen!
We have offended very grievously,
And been most tyrannous. From east to west
A groan of accusation pierces Heaven!
The wretched plead against us; multitudes   45
Countless and vehement, the sons of God,
Our brethren! Like a cloud that travels on,
Steamed up from Cairo's swamps of pestilence,
Even so, my countrymen! have we gone forth
And borne to distant tribes slavery and pangs,   50
And, deadlier far, our vices, whose deep taint
With slow perdition murders the whole man,
His body and his soul! Meanwhile, at home,
All individual dignity and power
Engulfed in Courts, Committees, Institutions,   55
Associations and Societies,
A vain, speech-mouthing, speech-reporting Guild,
One Benefit-Club for mutual flattery,
We have drunk up, demure as at a grace,

Pollutions from the brimming cup of wealth;   60
Contemptuous of all honourable rule,
Yet bartering freedom and the poor man's life
For gold, as at a market! The sweet words
Of Christian promise, words that even yet
Might stem destruction, were they wisely preached,   65
Are muttered o'er by men, whose tones proclaim
How flat and wearisome they feel their trade:
Rank scoffers some, but most too indolent
To deem them falsehoods or to know their truth.
Oh! blasphemous! the Book of Life is made   70
A superstitious instrument, on which
We gabble o'er the oaths we mean to break;
For all must swear – all and in every place,
College and wharf, council and justice-court;
All, all must swear, the briber and the bribed,   75
Merchant and lawyer, senator and priest,
The rich, the poor, the old man and the young;
All, all make up one scheme of perjury,
That faith doth reel; the very name of God
Sounds like a juggler's charm; and, bold with joy,   80
Forth from his dark and lonely hiding-place,
(Portentous sight!) the owlet Atheism,
Sailing on obscene wings athwart the noon,
Drops his blue-fringéd lids, and holds them close,
And hooting at the glorious sun in Heaven,   85
Cries out, 'Where is it?'
                       Thankless too for peace,
(Peace long preserved by fleets and perilous seas)
Secure from actual warfare, we have loved
To swell the war-whoop, passionate for war!
Alas! for ages ignorant of all   90
Its ghastlier workings, (famine or blue plague,
Battle, or siege, or flight through wintry snows),
We, this whole people, have been clamorous
For war and bloodshed; animating sports,
The which we pay for as a thing to talk of,   95
Spectators and not combatants! No guess
Anticipative of a wrong unfelt,
No speculation on contingency,

However dim and vague, too vague and dim
To yield a justifying cause; and forth,   100
(Stuffed out with big preamble, holy names,
And adjurations of the God in Heaven,)
We send our mandates for the certain death
Of thousands and ten thousands! Boys and girls,
And women, that would groan to see a child   105
Pull off an insect's leg, all read of war,
The best amusement for our morning-meal!
The poor wretch, who has learnt his only prayers
From curses, who knows scarcely words enough
To ask a blessing from his Heavenly Father,   110
Becomes a fluent phraseman, absolute
And technical in victories and defeats,
And all our dainty terms for fratricide;
Terms which we trundle smoothly o'er our tongues
Like mere abstractions, empty sounds to which   115
We join no feeling and attach no form!
As if the soldier died without a wound;
As if the fibres of this godlike frame
Were gored without a pang; as if the wretch,
Who fell in battle, doing bloody deeds,   120
Passed off to Heaven, translated and not killed;
As though he had no wife to pine for him,
No God to judge him! Therefore, evil days
Are coming on us, O my countrymen!
And what if all-avenging Providence,   125
Strong and retributive, should make us know
The meaning of our words, force us to feel
The desolation and the agony
Of our fierce doings?
                        Spare us yet awhile,
Father and God! O! spare us yet awhile!   130
Oh! let not English women drag their flight
Fainting beneath the burthen of their babes,
Of the sweet infants, that but yesterday
Laughed at the breast! Sons, brothers, husbands, all
Who ever gazed with fondness on the forms   135
Which grew up with you round the same fire-side,
And all who ever heard the sabbath-bells

Without the infidel's scorn, make yourselves pure!
Stand forth! be men! repel an impious foe,
Impious and false, a light yet cruel race,   140
Who laugh away all virtue, mingling mirth
With deeds of murder; and still promising
Freedom, themselves too sensual to be free,
Poison life's amities, and cheat the heart
Of faith and quiet hope, and all that soothes   145
And all that lifts the spirit! Stand we forth;
Render them back upon the insulted ocean,
And let them toss as idly on its waves
As the vile sea-weed, which some mountain-blast
Swept from our shores! and oh! may we return   150
Not with a drunken triumph, but with fear,
Repenting of the wrongs with which we stung
So fierce a foe to frenzy!
                    I have told,
O Britons! O my brethren! I have told
Most bitter truth, but without bitterness.   155
Nor deem my zeal or factious or mis-timed;
For never can true courage dwell with them,
Who, playing tricks with conscience, dare not look
At their own vices. We have been too long
Dupes of a deep delusion! Some, belike,   160
Groaning with restless enmity, expect
All change from change of constituted power;
As if a Government had been a robe.
On which our vice and wretchedness were tagged
Like fancy-points and fringes, with the robe,   165
Pulled off at pleasure. Fondly these attach
A radical causation to a few
Poor drudges of chastising Providence,
Who borrow all their hues and qualities
From our own folly and rank wickedness,   170
Which gave them birth and nursed them. Others, meanwhile,
Dote with a mad idolatry; and all
Who will not fall before their images,
And yield them worship, they are enemies
Even of their country!
                  Such have I been deemed –   175

But, O dear Britain! O my Mother Isle!
Needs must thou prove a name most dear and holy
To me, a son, a brother, and a friend,
A husband, and a father! who revere
All bonds of natural love, and find them all   180
Within the limits of thy rocky shores.
O native Britain! O my Mother Isle!
How shouldst thou prove aught else but dear and holy
To me, who from thy lakes and mountain-hills,
Thy clouds, thy quiet dales, thy rocks and seas,   185
Have drunk in all my intellectual life,
All sweet sensations, all ennobling thoughts,
All adoration of the God in nature,
All lovely and all honourable things,
Whatever makes this mortal spirit feel   190
The joy and greatness of its future being!
There lives nor form nor feeling in my soul
Unborrowed from my country! O divine
And beauteous island! thou hast been my sole
And most magnificent temple, in the which   195
I walk with awe, and sing my stately songs,
Loving the God that made me! –
                                        May my fears,
My filial fears, be vain! and may the vaunts
And menace of the vengeful enemy
Pass like the gust, that roared and died away   200
In the distant tree: which heard, and only heard
In this low dell, bowed not the delicate grass.

  But now the gentle dew-fall sends abroad
The fruit-like perfume of the golden furze:
The light has left the summit of the hill,   205
Though still a sunny gleam lies beautiful,
Aslant the ivied beacon. Now farewell,
Farewell, awhile, O soft and silent spot!
On the green sheep-track, up the heathy hill,
Homeward I wind my way; and lo! recalled   210
From bodings that have well nigh wearied me,
I find myself upon the brow, and pause
Startled! And after lonely sojourning

In such a quiet and surrounded nook,
This burst of prospect, here the shadowy main,   215
Dim tinted, there the mighty majesty
Of that huge amphitheatre of rich
And elmy fields, seems like society –
Conversing with the mind, and giving it
A livelier impulse and a dance of thought!   220
And now, belovéd Stowey! I behold
Thy church-tower, and, methinks, the four huge elms
Clustering, which mark the mansion of my friend;
And close behind them, hidden from my view,
Is my own lowly cottage, where my babe   225
And my babe's mother dwell in peace! With light
And quickened footsteps thitherward I tend,
Remembering thee, O green and silent dell!
And grateful, that by nature's quietness
And solitary musings, all my heart   230
Is softened, and made worthy to indulge
Love, and the thoughts that yearn for human kind.

NETHER STOWEY, 28 APRIL 1798

Christabel

PART I

'Tis the middle of night by the castle clock,
And the owls have awakened the crowing cock;
Tu—whit!——Tu—whoo!
And hark, again! the crowing cock,
How drowsily it crew,   5

Sir Leoline, the Baron rich,
Hath a toothless mastiff bitch;
From her kennel beneath the rock
She maketh answer to the clock,
Four for the quarters, and twelve for the hour;   10
Ever and aye, by shine and shower,

Sixteen short howls, not over loud;
Some say, she sees my lady's shroud.

Is the night chilly and dark?
The night is chilly, but not dark.   15
The thin gray cloud is spread on high,
It covers but not hides the sky.
The moon is behind, and at the full;
And yet she looks both small and dull.
The night is chill, the cloud is gray: 20
'Tis a month before the month of May,
And the Spring comes slowly up this way.

The lovely lady, Christabel,
Whom her father loves so well,
What makes her in the wood so late,   25
A furlong from the castle gate?
She had dreams all yesternight
Of her own betrothéd knight;
And she in the midnight wood will pray
For the weal of her lover that's far away.   30

She stole along, she nothing spoke,
The sighs she heaved were soft and low,
And naught was green upon the oak
But moss and rarest mistletoe:
She kneels beneath the huge oak tree,   35
And in silence prayeth she.

The lady sprang up suddenly,
The lovely lady, Christabel!
It moaned as near, as near can be,
But what it is she cannot tell. –   40
On the other side it seems to be,
Of the huge, broad-breasted, old oak tree.

The night is chill; the forest bare;
Is it the wind that moaneth bleak?
There is not wind enough in the air   45
To move away the ringlet curl

From the lovely lady's cheek –
There is not wind enough to twirl
The one red leaf, the last of its clan,
That dances as often as dance it can, 50
Hanging so light, and hanging so high,
On the topmost twig that looks up at the sky.

Hush, beating heart of Christabel!
Jesu, Maria, shield her well!
She folded her arms beneath her cloak, 55
And stole to the other side of oak.
        What sees she there?

There she sees a damsel bright,
Drest in a silken robe of white,
That shadowy in the moonlight shone: 60
The neck that made that white robe wan,
Her stately neck, and arms were bare;
Her blue-veined feet unsandal'd were,
And wildly glittered here and there
The gems entangled in her hair. 65
I guess, 'twas frightful there to see
A lady so richly clad as she –
Beautiful exceedingly!

Mary mother, save me now!
(Said Christabel,) And who art thou? 70

The lady strange made answer meet,
And her voice was faint and sweet: –
Have pity on my sore distress,
I scarce can speak for weariness:
Stretch forth thy hand, and have no fear! 75
Said Christabel, How camest thou here?
And the lady, whose voice was faint and sweet,
Did thus pursue her answer meet:–

My sire is of a noble line,
And my name is Geraldine: 80
Five warriors seized me yestermorn,
Me, even me, a maid forlorn:

They choked my cries with force and fright,
And tied me on a palfrey white.
The palfrey was as fleet as wind,   85
And they rode furiously behind.
They spurred amain, their steeds were white:
And once we crossed the shade of night.
As sure as Heaven shall rescue me,
I have no thought what men they be;   90
Nor do I know how long it is
(For I have lain entranced I wis)
Since one, the tallest of the five,
Took me from the palfrey's back,
A weary woman, scarce alive.   95
Some muttered words his comrades spoke:
He placed me underneath this oak;
He swore they would return with haste;
Whither they went I cannot tell –
I thought I heard, some minutes past,   100
Sounds as of a castle bell.
Stretch forth thy hand (thus ended she),
And help a wretched maid to flee.

Then Christabel stretched forth her hand,
And comforted fair Geraldine: 105
O well, bright dame! may you command
The service of Sir Leoline;
And gladly our stout chivalry
Will he send forth and friends withal
To guide and guard you safe and free   110
Home to your noble father's hall.

She rose: and forth with steps they passed
That strove to be, and were not, fast.
Her gracious stars the lady blest,
And thus spake on sweet Christabel: 115
All our household are at rest,
The hall as silent as the cell;
Sir Leoline is weak in health,
And may not well awakened be,
But we will move as if in stealth,   120

And I beseech your courtesy,
This night, to share your couch with me.

They crossed the moat, and Christabel
Took the key that fitted well;
A little door she opened straight,   125
All in the middle of the gate;
The gate that was ironed within and without,
Where an army in battle array had marched out.
The lady sank, belike through pain,
And Christabel with might and main   130
Lifted her up, a weary weight,
Over the threshold of the gate:
Then the lady rose again,
And moved, as she were not in pain.

So free from danger, free from fear,   135
They crossed the court: right glad they were.
And Christabel devoutly cried
To the lady by her side,
Praise we the Virgin all divine
Who hath rescued thee from thy distress!   140
Alas, alas! said Geraldine,
I cannot speak for weariness.
So free from danger, free from fear,
They crossed the court: right glad they were.

Outside her kennel, the mastiff old   145
Lay fast asleep, in moonshine cold.
The mastiff old did not awake,
Yet she an angry moan did make!
And what can ail the mastiff bitch?
Never till now she uttered yell   150
Beneath the eye of Christabel.
Perhaps it is the owlet's scritch:
For what can ail the mastiff bitch?

They passed the hall, that echoes still,
Pass as lightly as you will!   155
The brands were flat, the brands were dying,

Amid their own white ashes lying;
But when the lady passed, there came
A tongue of light, a fit of flame;
And Christabel saw the lady's eye,   160
And nothing else saw she thereby,
Save the boss of the shield of Sir Leoline tall,
Which hung in a murky old niche in the wall.
O softly tread, said Christabel,
My father seldom sleepeth well.   165

Sweet Christabel her feet doth bare,
And jealous of the listening air
They steal their way from stair to stair,
Now in glimmer, and now in gloom,
And now they pass the Baron's room,   170
As still as death, with stifled breath!
And now have reached her chamber door;
And now doth Geraldine press down
The rushes of the chamber floor.

The moon shines dim in the open air,   175
And not a moonbeam enters here.
But they without its light can see
The chamber carved so curiously,
Carved with figures strange and sweet,
All made out of the carver's brain,   180
For a lady's chamber meet:
The lamp with twofold silver chain
Is fastened to an angel's feet.

The silver lamp burns dead and dim;
But Christabel the lamp will trim.   185
She trimmed the lamp, and made it bright,
And left it swinging to and fro,
While Geraldine, in wretched plight,
Sank down upon the floor below.

O weary lady, Geraldine,   190
I pray you, drink this cordial wine!

It is a wine of virtuous powers;
My mother made it of wild flowers.

And will your mother pity me,
Who am a maiden most forlorn?   195
Christabel answered – Woe is me!
She died the hour that I was born.
I have heard the grey-haired friar tell
How on her death-bed she did say,
That she should hear the castle-bell   200
Strike twelve upon my wedding-day.
O mother dear! that thou wert here!
I would, said Geraldine, she were!

But soon with altered voice, said she –
'Off, wandering mother! Peak and pine!   205
I have power to bid thee flee.'
Alas! what ails poor Geraldine?
Why stares she with unsettled eye?
Can she the bodiless dead espy?
And why with hollow voice cries she,   210
'Off, woman, off! this hour is mine –
Though thou her guardian spirit be,
Off, woman, off! 'tis given to me.'

Then Christabel knelt by the lady's side,
And raised to heaven her eyes so blue –   215
Alas! said she, this ghastly ride –
Dear lady! it hath wildered you!
The lady wiped her moist cold brow,
And faintly said, ''Tis over now!'

Again the wild-flower wine she drank: 220
Her fair large eyes 'gan glitter bright,
And from the floor whereon she sank,
The lofty lady stood upright:
She was most beautiful to see,
Like a lady of a far countrée.   225

And thus the lofty lady spake –
'All they who live in the upper sky,
Do love you, holy Christabel!

And you love them, and for their sake
And for the good which me befel,   230
Even I in my degree will try,
Fair maiden, to requite you well.
But now unrobe yourself; for I
Must pray, ere yet in bed I lie.'

Quoth Christabel, so let it be!   235
And as the lady bade, did she.
Her gentle limbs did she undress,
And lay down in her loveliness.

But through her brain of weal and woe
So many thoughts moved to and fro,   240
That vain it were her lids to close;
So half-way from the bed she rose,
And on her elbow did recline
To look at the lady Geraldine.

Beneath the lamp the lady bowed,   245
And slowly rolled her eyes around;
Then drawing in her breath aloud,
Like one that shuddered, she unbound
The cincture from beneath her breast:
Her silken robe, and inner vest,   250
Dropt to her feet, and full in view,
Behold! her bosom and half her side –[1]
A sight to dream of, not to tell!
O shield her! shield sweet Christabel!

Yet Geraldine nor speaks nor stirs;   255
Ah! what a stricken look was hers!
Deep from within she seems half-way
To lift some weight with sick assay,
And eyes the maid and seeks delay;
Then suddenly, as one defied,   260
Collects herself in scorn and pride,
And lay down by the Maiden's side! –

[1] In at least one copy this line is followed by another, pencilled in by Coleridge:
'It was dark & rough as the Sea-Wolf's hide.'

And in her arms the maid she took,
  Ah wel-a-day!
And with low voice and doleful look   265
These words did say:
'In the touch of this bosom there worketh a spell,
Which is lord of thy utterance, Christabel!
Thou knowest to-night, and wilt know to-morrow
This mark of my shame, this seal of my sorrow; 270
  But vainly thou warrest,
   For this is alone in
  Thy power to declare
   That in the dim forest
  Thou heard'st a low moaning,   275
And found'st a bright lady, surpassingly fair;
And didst bring her home with thee in love and
  in charity,
To shield her and shelter her from the damp air.'

THE CONCLUSION TO PART I

It was a lovely sight to see
The lady Christbel, when she   280
Was praying at the old oak tree.
  Amid the jaggéd shadows
  Of mossy leafless boughs,
  Kneeling in the moonlight,
  To make her gentle vows;   285
Her slender palms together prest,
Heaving sometimes on her breast;
Her face resigned to bliss or bale –
Her face, oh call it fair not pale,
And both blue eyes more bright than clear, 290
Each about to have a tear.

With open eyes (ah woe is me!)
Asleep, and dreaming fearfully,
Fearfully dreaming, yet, I wis,
Dreaming that alone, which is –   295
O sorrow and shame! Can this be she,
The lady, who knelt at the old oak tree?
And lo! the worker of these harms,

That holds the maiden in her arms,
Seems to slumber still and mild,   300
As a mother with her child.

A star hath set, a star hath risen,
O Geraldine! since arms of thine
Have been the lovely lady's prison.
O Geraldine! one hour was thine –   305
Thou'st had thy will! By tairn[1] and rill,
The night-birds all that hour were still.
But now they are jubilant anew,
From cliff and tower, tu—whoo! tu—whoo!
Tu—whoo! tu—whoo! from wood and fell!   310

And see! the lady Christabel
Gathers herself from out her trance;
Her limbs relax, her countenance
Grows sad and soft; the smooth thin lids
Close o'er her eyes; and tears she sheds –   315
Large tears that leave the lashes bright!
And oft the while she seems to smile
As infants at a sudden light!

Yea, she doth smile, and she doth weep,
Like a youthful hermitess,   320
Beauteous in a wilderness,
Who, praying always, prays in sleep.
And, if she move unquietly,
Perchance, 'tis but the blood so free
Comes back and tingles in her feet.   325
No doubt, she hath a vision sweet.
What if her guardian spirit 'twere,
What if she knew her mother near?
But this she knows, in joys and woes,

[1] Tairn or Tarn (derived by Lye from the Icelandic *Tiorn*, stagnum, palus) is rendered in our dictionaries as synonymous with Mere or Lake; but it is properly a large Pool or Reservoir in the Mountains, commonly the Feeder of some Mere in the valleys. Tarn Watling and Blellum Tarn, though on lower ground than other Tarns, are yet not exceptions, for both are on elevations, and Blellum Tarn feeds the Wynander Mere. [S.T.C.]

That saints will aid if men will call: 330
For the blue sky bends over all!
[1797]

PART II

Each matin bell, the Baron saith,
Knells us back to a world of death.
These words Sir Leoline first said,
When he rose and found his lady dead: 335
These words Sir Leoline will say
Many a morn to his dying day!

And hence the custom and law began
That still at dawn the sacristan,
Who duly pulls the heavy bell,   340
Five and forty beads must tell
Between each stroke – a warning knell,
Which not a soul can choose but hear
From Bratha Head to Wyndermere.

Saith Bracy the bard, So let it knell!   345
And let the drowsy sacristan
Still count as slowly as he can!
There is no lack of such, I ween,
As well fill up the space between.
In Langdale Pike and Witch's Lair,   350
And Dungeon-ghyll so foully rent,
With ropes of rock and bells of air
Three sinful sextons' ghosts are pent,
Who all give back, one after t'other,
The death-note to their living brother;   355
And oft too, by the knell offended,
Just as their one! two! three! is ended,
The devil mocks the doleful tale
With a merry peal from Borodale.

The air is still! through mist and cloud   360
That merry peal comes ringing loud;
And Geraldine shakes off her dread,

And rises lightly from the bed;
Puts on her silken vestments white,
And tricks her hair in lovely plight,   365
And nothing doubting of her spell
Awakens the lady Christabel.
'Sleep you, sweet lady Christabel?
I trust that you have rested well.'

And Christabel awoke and spied   370
The same who lay down by her side –
O rather say, the same whom she
Raised up beneath the old oak tree!
Nay, fairer yet! and yet more fair!
For she belike hath drunken deep   375
Of all the blessedness of sleep!
And while she spake, her looks, her air
Such gentle thankfulness declare,
That (so it seemed) her girded vests
Grew tight beneath her heaving breasts.   380
'Sure I have sinn'd!' said Christabel.
'Now heaven be praised if all be well!'
And in low faltering tones, yet sweet,
Did she the lofty lady greet
With such perplexity of mind   385
As dreams too lively leave behind.

So quickly she rose, and quickly arrayed
Her maiden limbs, and having prayed
That He, who on the cross did groan,
Might wash away her sins unknown,   390
She forthwith led fair Geraldine
To meet her sire, Sir Leoline.

The lovely maid and the lady tall
Are pacing both into the hall,
And pacing on through page and groom,   395
Enter the Baron's presence-room.

The Baron rose, and while he prest
His gentle daughter to his breast,
With cheerful wonder in his eyes

The lady Geraldine espies,   400
And gave such welcome to the same,
As might beseem so bright a dame!

But when he heard the lady's tale,
And when she told her father's name,
Why waxed Sir Leoline so pale,   405
Murmuring o'er the name again,
Lord Roland de Vaux of Tryermaine?

Alas! they had been friends in youth;
But whispering tongues can poison truth;
And constancy lives in realms above;   410
And life is thorny; and youth is vain;
And to be wroth with one we love
Doth work like madness in the brain.
And thus it chanced, as I divine,
With Roland and Sir Leoline.   415
Each spake words of high disdain
And insult to his heart's best brother:
They parted – ne'er to meet again!
But never either found another
To free the hollow heart from paining –   420
They stood aloof, the scars remaining,
Like cliffs, which had been rent asunder;
A dreary sea now flows between; –
But neither heat, nor frost, nor thunder,
Shall wholly do away, I ween,   425
The marks of that which once hath been.

Sir Leoline, a moment's space,
Stood gazing on the damsel's face:
And the youthful Lord of Tryermaine
Came back upon his heart again.   430

O then the Baron forgot his age,
His noble heart swelled high with rage;
He swore by the wounds in Jesu's side,
He would proclaim it far and wide
With trump and solemn heraldry,   435

That they, who thus had wronged the dame,
Were base as spotted infamy!
'And if they dare deny the same,
My herald shall appoint a week,
And let the recreant traitors seek .   440
My tourney court – that there and then
I may dislodge their reptile souls
From the bodies and forms of men!'
He spake: his eye in lightning rolls!
For the lady was ruthlessly seized; and he kenned   445
In the beautiful lady the child of his friend!

And now the tears were on his face,
And fondly in his arms he took
Fair Geraldine, who met the embrace,
Prolonging it with joyous look.   450
Which when she viewed, a vision fell
Upon the soul of Christabel,
The vision of fear, the touch and pain!
She shrunk and shuddered, and saw again –
(Ah, woe is me! Was it for thee,   455
Thou gentle maid! such sights to see?)

Again she saw that bosom old,
Again she felt that bosom cold,
And drew in her breath with a hissing sound:
Whereat the Knight turned wildly round,   460
And nothing saw, but his own sweet maid
With eyes upraised, as one that prayed.

The touch, the sight, had passed away,
And in its stead that vision blest,
Which comforted her after-rest,   465
While in the lady's arms she lay,
Had put a rapture in her breast,
And on her lips and o'er her eyes
Spread smiles like light!
                          With new surprise,
'What ails then my belovéd child?'   470
The Baron said – His daughter mild

Made answer, 'All will yet be well!'
I ween, she had no power to tell
Aught else: so mighty was the spell.

Yet he, who saw this Geraldine,   475
Had deemed her sure a thing divine,
Such sorrow with such grace she blended,
As if she feared, she had offended
Sweet Christabel, that gentle maid!
And with such lowly tones she prayed,   480
She might be sent without delay
Home to her father's mansion.
                                        'Nay!
Nay, by my soul!' said Leoline.
'Ho! Bracy the bard, the charge be thine!
Go thou, with music sweet and loud   485
And take two steeds with trappings proud,
And take the youth whom thou lov'st best
To bear thy harp, and learn thy song,
And clothe you both in solemn vest,
And over the mountains haste along,   490
Lest wandering folk, that are abroad,
Detain you on the valley road.

'And when he has crossed the Irthing flood,
My merry bard! he hastes, he hastes
Up Knorren Moor, through Halegarth Wood,   495
And reaches soon that castle good
Which stands and threatens Scotland's wastes.

'Bard Bracy! bard Bracy! your horses are fleet,
Ye must ride up the hall, your music so sweet,
More loud than your horses' echoing feet!   500
And loud and loud to Lord Roland call,
Thy daughter is safe in Langdale hall!
Thy beautiful daughter is safe and free –
Sir Leoline greets thee thus through me.
He bids thee come without delay   505
With all thy numerous array

And take thy lovely daughter home:
And he will meet thee on the way
With all his numerous array
White with their panting palfreys' foam: 510
And, by mine honour! I will say,
That I repent me of the day
When I spake words of fierce disdain
To Roland de Vaux of Tryermaine! –
– For since that evil hour hath flown,   515
Many a summer's sun hath shone;
Yet ne'er found I a friend again
Like Roland de Vaux of Tryermaine.'

The lady fell, and clasped his knees,
Her face upraised, her eyes o'erflowing;   520
And Bracy replied, with faltering voice,
His gracious Hail on all bestowing! –
'Thy words, thou sire of Christabel,
Are sweeter than my harp can tell;
Yet might I gain a boon of thee,   525
This day my journey should not be,
So strange a dream hath come to me,
That I had vowed with music loud
To clear yon wood from thing unblest,
Warned by a vision in my rest!   530
For in my sleep I saw that dove,
That gentle bird, whom thou dost love,
And call'st by thy own daughter's name –
Sir Leoline! I saw the same
Fluttering, and uttering fearful moan,   535
Among the green herbs in the forest alone.
Which when I saw and when I heard,
I wonder'd what might ail the bird;
For nothing near it could I see,
Save the grass and green herbs underneath the old tree. 540

'And in my dream methought I went
To search out what might there be found;
And what the sweet bird's trouble meant,

That thus lay fluttering on the ground.
I went and peered, and could descry   545
No cause for her distressful cry;
But yet for her dear lady's sake
I stooped, methought, the dove to take,
When lo! I saw a bright green snake
Coiled around its wings and neck.   550
Green as the herbs on which it couched,
Close by the dove's its head it crouched;
And with the dove it heaves and stirs,
Swelling its neck as she swelled hers!
I woke; it was the midnight hour,   555
The clock was echoing in the tower;
But though my slumber was gone by,
This dream it would not pass away –
It seems to live upon my eye!
And thence I vowed this self-same day,   560
With music strong and saintly song
To wander through the forest bare,
Lest aught unholy loiter there.'

Thus Bracy said: the Baron, the while,
Half-listening heard him with a smile;   565
Then turned to Lady Geraldine,
His eyes made up of wonder and love;
And said in courtly accents fine,
'Sweet maid, Lord Roland's beauteous dove,
With arms more strong than harp or song,   570
Thy sire and I will crush the snake!'
He kissed her forehead as he spake,
And Geraldine in maiden wise,
Casting down her large bright eyes,
With blushing cheek and courtesy fine   575
She turned her from Sir Leoline;
Softly gathering up her train,
That o'er her right arm fell again;
And folded her arms across her chest,
And couched her head upon her breast,   580

And looked askance at Christabel –
Jesu, Maria, shield her well!

A snake's small eye blinks dull and shy,
And the lady's eyes they shrunk in her head,
Each shrunk up to a serpent's eye,   585
And with somewhat of malice, and more of dread,
At Christabel she looked askance! –
One moment – and the sight was fled!
But Christabel in dizzy trance
Stumbling on the unsteady ground   590
Shuddered aloud, with a hissing sound;
And Geraldine again turned round,
And like a thing, that sought relief,
Full of wonder and full of grief,
She rolled her large bright eyes divine   595
Wildly on Sir Leoline.

The maid, alas! her thoughts are gone,
She nothing sees – no sight but one!
The maid, devoid of guile and sin,
I know not how, in fearful wise,   600
So deeply had she drunken in
That look, those shrunken serpent eyes,
That all her features were resigned
To this sole image in her mind:
And passively did imitate   605
That look of dull and treacherous hate!
And thus she stood, in dizzy trance,
Still picturing that look askance
With forced unconscious sympathy
Full before her father's view –   610
As far as such a look could be,
In eyes so innocent and blue!

And when the trance was o'er, the maid
Paused awhile, and inly prayed:
Then falling at the Baron's feet,   615
'By my mother's soul do I entreat
That thou this woman send away!'
She said: and more she could not say:

For what she knew she could not tell,
O'er-mastered by the mighty spell. 620

Why is thy cheek so wan and wild,
Sir Leoline? Thy only child
Lies at thy feet, thy joy, thy pride,
So fair, so innocent, so mild;
The same, for whom thy lady died! 625
O by the pangs of her dear mother
Think thou no evil of thy child!
For her, and thee, and for no other,
She prayed the moment ere she died:
Prayed that the babe for whom she died, 630
Might prove her dear lord's joy and pride!
    That prayer her deadly pangs beguiled,
        Sir Leoline!
    And wouldst thou wrong thy only child,
        Her child and thine? 635

Within the Baron's heart and brain
If thoughts, like these, had any share,
They only swelled his rage and pain,
And did but work confusion there.
His heart was cleft with pain and rage, 640
His cheeks they quivered, his eyes were wild,
Dishonoured thus in his old age;
Dishonoured by his only child,
And all this hospitality
To the wronged daughter of his friend 645
By more than woman's jealousy
Brought thus to a disgraceful end –
He rolled his eye with stern regard
Upon the gentle minstrel bard,
And said in tones abrupt, austere – 650
'Why, Bracy! dost thou loiter here?
I bade thee hence!' The bard obeyed;
And turning from his own sweet maid,
The agéd knight, Sir Leoline,
Led forth the lady Geraldine! 655

[1800]

THE CONCLUSION TO PART II

A little child, a limber elf,
Singing, dancing to itself,
A fairy thing with red round cheeks,
That always finds, and never seeks,
Makes such a vision to the sight   660
As fills a father's eyes with light;
And pleasures flow in so thick and fast
Upon his heart, that he at last
Must needs express his love's excess
With words of unmeant bitterness.   665
Perhaps 'tis pretty to force together
Thoughts so all unlike each other;
To mutter and mock a broken charm,
To dally with wrong that does no harm.
Perhaps 'tis tender too and pretty   670
At each wild word to feel within
A sweet recoil of love and pity.
And what, if in a world of sin
(O sorrow and shame should this be true!)
Such giddiness of heart and brain   675
Comes seldom save from rage and pain,
So talks as it's most used to do.

Love

All thoughts, all passions, all delights
Whatever stirs this mortal frame,
All are but ministers of Love,
    And feed his sacred flame.

Oft in my waking dreams do I   5
Live o'er again that happy hour,
When midway on the mount I lay,
    Beside the ruined tower.

The moonshine, stealing o'er the scene,
Had blended with the lights of eve;   10
And she was there, my hope, my joy,
    My own dear Genevieve!

She leant against the arméd man,
The statue of the arméd knight;[1]
She stood and listened to my lay,   15
    Amid the lingering light.

Few sorrows hath she of her own,
My hope! my joy! my Genevieve!
She loves me best, whene'er I sing
    The songs that make her grieve.   20

I played a soft and doleful air,
I sang an old and moving story –
An old rude song, that suited well,
    That ruin wild and hoary.

She listened with a flitting blush,   25
With downcast eyes and modest grace;
For well she knew, I could not choose
    But gaze upon her face.

I told her of the Knight that wore
Upon his shield a burning brand;   30
And that for ten long years he wooed
    The Lady of the Land.

I told her how he pined: and ah!
The deep, the low, the pleading tone

[1] In the church at Sockburn there is a recumbent statue of an 'armed knight' . . . and in a field near the farm-house there is a 'Grey-Stone' which is said to commemorate the slaying of a monstrous wyverne or 'worme' by the knight who is buried in the church. It is difficult to believe that the 'armed knight' and the 'grey stone' of the first draft were not suggested by the statue in Sockburn Church, and the 'Grey-Stone' in the adjoining field. [E.H.C.] It was while on a visit to Sockburn in 1799 that Coleridge fell in love with Sara Hutchinson, and E.H.C. no doubt had this in mind. [Ed.]

With which I sang another's love,   35
    Interpreted my own.

She listened with a flitting blush,
With downcast eyes, and modest grace;
And she forgave me, that I gazed
    Too fondly on her face!   40

But when I told the cruel scorn
That crazed that bold and lovely Knight,
And that he crossed the mountain-woods,
    Nor rested day nor night;

That sometimes from the savage den,   45
And sometimes from the darksome shade,
And sometimes starting up at once
    In green and sunny glade, –

There came and looked him in the face
An angel beautiful and bright;   50
And that he knew it was a Fiend,
    This miserable Knight!

And that unknowing what he did,
He leaped amid a murderous band,
And saved from outrage worse than death   55
    The Lady of the Land!

And how she wept, and clasped his knees;
And how she tended him in vain –
And ever strove to expiate
    The scorn that crazed his brain; –   60

And that she nursed him in a cave;
And how his madness went away,
And on the yellow forest-leaves
    A dying man he lay; –

His dying words – but when I reached   65
That tenderest strain of all the ditty,

My faultering voice and pausing harp
    Disturbed her soul with pity!

All impulses of soul and sense
Had thrilled my guileless Genevieve;   70
The music and the doleful tale,
    The rich and balmy eve;

And hopes, and fears that kindle hope,
An undistinguishable throng,
And gentle wishes long subdued,   75
    Subdued and cherished long!

She wept with pity and delight,
She blushed with love, and virgin-shame;
And like the murmur of a dream,
    I heard her breathe my name.   80

Her bosom heaved – she stepped aside,
As conscious of my look she stepped –
Then suddenly, with timorous eye
    She fled to me and wept.

She half enclosed me with her arms,   85
She pressed me with a meek embrace;
And bending back her head, looked up,
    And gazed upon my face.

'Twas partly love, and partly fear,
And partly 'twas a bashful art,   90
That I might rather feel, than see,
    The swelling of her heart.

I calmed her fears, and she was calm,
And told her love with virgin pride;
And so I won my Genevieve,   95
    My bright and beauteous Bride.
[November–December 1799]

To Mr Pye[1]

On his *Carmen Seculare* (a title which has by various persons who have heard it, been thus translated, 'A Poem *an age long*').

> Your Poem must *eternal* be,
>   *Eternal!* it can't fail,
> For 'tis *incomprehensible*,
>   And without head or tail!
> [1799, published 1800]

To a Critic

Who extracted a passage from a poem without adding a word respecting the context, and then derided it as unintelligible

> Most candid critic, what if I,
> By way of joke, pull out your eye,
> And holding up the fragment, cry,
> 'Ha! ha! that men such fools should be!
> Behold this shapeless Dab! – and he
> Who own'd it, fancied it could *see!*'
> The joke were mighty analytic,
> But should you like it, candid critic?

[1] Later reprinted as 'To the Author of the Ancient Mariner'. Cf. Lessing's 'Die Ewigheit gewisser Gedichte'. [K.C.] The much ridiculed Poet Laureate, Henry James Pye, produced his 'Carmen Seculare for the year 1800' to commemorate the turn of the century. In Roman times a 'secular ode' celebrated the end of a 'saeculum' (100 years, or an 'age').

Letter to – [Sara Hutchinson][1]

4 April 1802 – Sunday evening

Well! if the Bard was weatherwise, who made
The grand old Ballad of Sir Patrick Spence,
This Night, so tranquil now, will not go hence
Unrous'd by winds, that ply a busier trade
Than that, which moulds yon clouds in lazy flakes,   5
Or the dull sobbing Draft, that drones & rakes
Upon the Strings of this Eolian Lute,
    Which better far were mute.
For, lo! the New Moon, winter-bright!
And overspread with phantom Light,   10
(With swimming phantom Light o'erspread
But rimm'd & circled with a silver Thread)
I see the Old Moon in her Lap, foretelling
The coming-on of Rain & squally Blast –
O! Sara! that the Gust ev'n now were swelling,   15
And the slant Night-shower driving loud & fast!

A Grief without a pang, void, dark & drear,
A stifling, drowsy, unimpassion'd Grief
That finds no natural Outlet, no Relief
    In word, or sigh, or tear –   20
This, Sara! well thou know'st,
Is that sore Evil, which I dread the most,
And oft'nest suffer! In this heartless Mood,
To other thoughts by yonder Throstle woo'd,
That pipes within the Larch tree, not unseen,   25
(The Larch, which pushes out in tassels green
It's bundled Leafits) woo'd to mild Delights
By all the tender Sounds & gentle Sights

[1] Having written this verse-letter orginally to Sara Hutchinson, Coleridge went on to produce several versions from which the private references were removed, including one which he published as *Dejection: An Ode* on 4 October 1802, Wordsworth's wedding day. In the shortened versions the recipient was named variously as 'Wordsworth', 'William' and 'Edmund'; the one for *Sibylline Leaves* (1817) is addressed to a 'Lady'. For a study of the various versions see David Pirie, 'A Letter to [Asra]' in *Bicentenary Wordsworth Studies*, ed. J. Wordsworth (1970).

Of this sweet Primrose-month – & *vainly* woo'd
O dearest Sara! in this heartless Mood   30
All this long Eve, so balmy & serene
Have I been gazing on the western Sky
And it's peculiar Tint of Yellow Green –
And still I gaze – & with how blank an eye!
And those thin Clouds above, in flakes & bars,   35
That give away their Motion to the Stars;
Those Stars, that glide behind them, or between,
Now sparkling, now bedimm'd, but always seen;
Yon crescent Moon, as fix'd as if it grew
In it's own cloudless, starless Lake of Blue –   40
A boat becalm'd! dear William's Sky Canoe![1]
– I see them all, so excellently fair!
I see, not feel, how beautiful they are.

    My genial Spirits fail –
    And what can these avail   45
To lift the smoth'ring Weight from off my Breast?
    It were a vain Endeavor,
    Tho' I should gaze for ever
On that Green Light, which lingers in the West!
I may not hope from outward Forms to win   50
The Passion & the Life, whose Fountains are within!
These lifeless Shapes, around, below, Above,
    O what can they impart?
When even the gentle Thought, that thou, my Love!
    Art gazing now, like me,   55
    And see'st the Heaven, I see –
Sweet Thought it is – yet feebly stirs my Heart!

    Feebly! O feebly! – Yet
    (I well remember it)
In my first Dawn of Youth that Fancy stole   60
With many secret Yearnings on my Soul.
At eve, sky-gazing in 'ecstatic fit'
(Alas! for cloister'd in a city School
The Sky was all, I knew, of Beautiful)
At the barr'd window often did I sit,   65
And oft upon the leaded School-roof lay,

[1] See Wordsworth's 'Peter Bell', ll. 17, 113.

   And to myself would say –
There does not live a Man so stripp'd of good affections
As not to love to see a Maiden's quiet Eyes
Uprais'd, and linking on sweet Dreams by dim Connections   70
To moon, or Evening Star, or glorious western Skies –
While yet a Boy, this Thought would so pursue me
That often it became a kind of vision to me!

   Sweet Thought! and dear of old
     To Hearts of finer Mould!   75
Ten thousand times by Friends & Lovers blest!
   I spake with rash Despair,
   And ere I was aware,
The weight was somewhat lifted from my Breast!
O Sara! in the weather-fended Wood,   80
Thy lov'd haunt! where the Stock-doves coo at Noon,
   I guess, that thou hast stood
And watch'd yon Crescent, & it's ghost-like Moon.
And yet, far rather in my present mood
I would, that thou'dst been sitting all this while   85
Upon the sod-built Seat of Camomile –
And tho' thy Robin may have ceas'd to sing,
Yet needs for *my* sake must thou love to hear
The Bee-hive murmuring near,
That ever-busy & most quiet Thing   90
Which I have heard at Midnight murmuring.

   I feel my spirit moved –
   And wheresoe'er thou be,
   O Sister! O Beloved!
   Those dear mild Eyes, that see   95
   Even now the Heaven, *I* see –
There is a Prayer in them! It is for *me* –
And I, dear Sara – *I* am blessing *thee*!

It was as calm as this, that happy night
When Mary, thou, & I together were,   100
The low decaying Fire our only light,
And listen'd to the Stillness of the Air!
O that affectionate & blameless Maid,

Dear Mary! on her Lap my head she lay'd –
  Her Hand was on my Brow,   105
  Even as my own is now;
And on my Cheek I felt thy eye-lash play,
Such Joy I had, that I may truly say,
My Spirit was awe-stricken with the Excess
And trance-like Depth of it's brief Happiness.   110

Ah fair Remembrances, that so revive
The Heart, & fill it with a living Power,
Where were they, Sara? – or did I not strive
To win them to me? – on the fretting Hour
Then when I wrote thee that complaining Scroll   115
Which even to bodily Sickness bruis'd thy Soul!
And yet thou blam'st thyself alone! And yet
  Forbidd'st me all Regret!

And must I not regret, that I distress'd
Thee, best belov'd! who lovest me the best?   120
My better mind had fled, I know not whither,
For O! was this an Absent Friend's Employ
To send from far both Pain & Sorrow thither
  Where still his Blessings should have call'd down Joy!
I read thy guileless Letter o'er again –   125
I hear thee of thy blameless Self complain –
And only this I learn – & this, alas! I know –
That thou art weak & pale with Sickness, Grief & Pain –
  And I – I made thee so!

O for my own sake I regret perforce   130
Whatever turns thee, Sara! from the Course
Of calm Well-being & a Heart at rest!
When thou, & with thee those, whom thou lov'st best,
Shall dwell together in one happy Home,
One House, the dear *abiding* Home of All,   135
I too will crown me with a Coronal –
Nor shall this Heart in idle Wishes roam
  Morbidly soft!
No! let me trust, that I shall wear away
In no inglorious Toils the manly Day,   140

And only now & then, & not too oft,
Some dear & memorable Eve will bless
Dreaming of all your Loves & Quietness.

Be happy, & I need thee not in sight.
Peace in thy Heart, & Quiet in thy Dwelling, 145
Health in thy Limbs, & in thine Eyes the Light
Of Love, & Hope, & honorable Feeling –
Where e'er I am, I shall be well content!
Not near thee, haply shall be more content!
To all things I prefer the Permanent. 150

And better seems it for a heart, like mine,
Always to *know*, than sometimes to behold,
   Their Happiness & thine –
For Change doth trouble me with pangs untold!
To see thee, hear thee, feel thee – then to part 155
   Oh! it weighs down the Heart!
To *visit* those, I love, as I love thee,
Mary, & William, & dear Dorothy,
It is but a temptation to repine –
The transientness is Poison in the Wine, 160
Eats out the pith of joy, makes all Joy hollow,
All Pleasure a dim Dream of Pain to follow!
My own peculiar Lot, my house-hold Life
It is, & will remain, Indifference or Strife –
While *ye* are *well* & *happy*, 'twould but wrong you 165
If I should fondly yearn to be among you –
Wherefore, O wherefore! should I wish to be
A wither'd branch upon a blossoming Tree?

But (let me say it! for I vainly strive
To beat away the Thought) but if thou pin'd, 170
Whate'er the Cause, in body or in mind,
I were the miserablest Man alive
To know it & be absent! Thy Delights
Far off, or near, alike I may partake –
But O! to mourn for thee, & to forsake 175
All power, all hope of giving comfort to thee –
To know that thou art weak & worn with pain,

And not to hear thee, Sara! not to view thee –
   Not to sit beside thy Bed,
   Not press thy aching Head,   180
   Not bring thee Health again –
   At least to hope, to try –
By this Voice, which thou lov'st, & by this earnest Eye –

Nay, wherefore did I let it haunt my Mind
   The dark distressful Dream!   185
I turn from it, & listen to the Wind
Which long has rav'd unnotic'd! What a Scream
Of agony by Torture lengthen'd out
That Lute sent forth! O thou wild Storm without!
Jagg'd Rock, or mountain Pond, or blasted Tree,   190
Or Pine-Grove, whither Woodman never clomb,
Or lonely House, long held the Witches's Home,
Methinks were fitter Instruments for Thee,
Mad Lutanist! that in this month of Showers,
Of dark brown Gardens, & of peeping Flowers,   195
Mak'st Devil's Yule, with worse than wintry Song
The Blossoms, Buds, and timorous Leaves among!

Thou Actor, perfect in all tragic Sounds!
Thou mighty Poet, even to frenzy bold!
   What tell'st thou now about?   200
'Tis of the Rushing of an Host in Rout –
And many Groans from men with smarting Wounds –
At once they groan with smart, and shudder with the Cold!
'Tis hush'd! there is a Trance of deepest Silence,
Again! but all that Sound, as of a rushing Crowd,   205
And Groans & tremulous Shudderings, all are over –
And it has other Sounds, and all less deep, less loud!

   A Tale of less Affright,
   And temper'd with Delight,
As William's Self had made the tender Lay –   210
   'Tis of a little Child
   Upon a heathy Wild,
Not far from home – but it has lost it's way –

And now moans low in utter grief & fear –
And now screams loud, & hopes to make it's Mother hear!   215

'Tis Midnight! and small Thoughts have I of Sleep –
Full seldom may my Friend such Vigils keep –
O breathe She softly in her gentle Sleep!
Cover her, gentle Sleep! with wings of Healing.
And be this Tempest but a Mountain Birth!   220
May all the Stars hang bright about her Dwelling,
Silent, as tho' they *watch'd* the sleeping Earth!
Healthful & light, my Darling! may'st thou rise
    With clear & chearful Eyes –
And of the same good Tidings to me send!   225
    For, oh! beloved Friend!
I am not the buoyant Thing, I was of yore –
When, like an own Child, I to JOY belong'd;
For others mourning oft, myself oft sorely wrong'd,
Yet bearing all things then, as if I nothing bore!   230

    Yes, dearest Sara! Yes!
There *was* a time when tho' my path was rough,
The Joy within me dallied with Distress;
And all Misfortunes were but as the Stuff
Whence Fancy made me Dreams of Happiness: 235
For Hope grew round me, like the climbing Vine,
And Leaves & Fruitage, not my own, seem'd mine!
But now Ill Tidings bow me down to earth –
Nor care I, that they rob me of my Mirth –
    But oh! each Visitation   240
Suspends what Nature gave me at my Birth,
    My shaping Spirit of Imagination!
I speak not now of those habitual Ills
That wear out Life, when two unequal Minds
Meet in one House, & two discordant Wills –   245
    This leaves me, where it finds,
Past cure, & past Complaint – a fate austere
Too fix'd & hopeless to partake of Fear!

But thou, dear Sara! (dear indeed thou art,
My Comforter! A Heart within my Heart!)   250
Thou, & the Few, we love, tho' few ye be,

Make up a world of Hopes & Fears for me.
And if Affliction, or distemp'ring Pain,
Or wayward Chance befall you, I complain
Not that I mourn – O Friends, most dear! most true!   255
    Methinks to weep with you
Were better far than to rejoice alone –
But that my coarse domestic Life has known
No Habits of heart-nursing Sympathy,
No Griefs, but such as dull and deaden me,   260
No mutual mild Enjoyments of it's own,
No Hopes of its own Vintage. None, O! none –
Whence when I mourn'd for you, my Heart might borrow
Fair forms & living Motions for it's Sorrow.
For not to think of what I needs must feel,   265
But to be still & patient all I can;
And haply by abstruse Research to steal
From my own Nature all the Natural Man –
This was my sole Resource, my wisest plan!
And that, which suits a part, infects the whole,   270
And now is almost grown the Temper of my Soul.

My Little Children are a Joy, a Love,
    A good Gift from above!
But what is Bliss, that still calls up a Woe,
    And makes it doubly keen   275
Compelling me to *feel*, a well as KNOW,
What a most blessed Lot mine might have been.
Those little Angel Children (woe is me!)
There have been hours, when feeling how they bind
And pluck out the Wing-feathers of my Mind,   280
Turning my Error to Necessity,
I have half-wish'd, they never had been born!
That seldom! But sad Thoughts they always bring,
And like the Poet's Philomel, I sing
My Love-song, with my breast against a Thorn.   285

With no unthankful Spirit I confess,
This clinging Grief too, in it's turn, awakes
That Love, and Father's Joy; but O! it makes
The Love the greater, & the Joy far less.
These Mountains too, these Vales, these Woods, these Lakes,   290

Scenes full of Beauty & of Loftiness
Where all my Life I fondly hop'd to live –
I were sunk low indeed, did they *no* solace give;
But oft I seem to feel, & evermore I fear,
They are not to me now the Things, which once they were.   295

O Sara! we receive but what we give,
And in *our* Life alone does Nature live.
Our's is her Wedding Garment, our's her Shroud –
And would we aught behold of higher Worth
Than that inanimate cold World allow'd   300
To the poor loveless ever-anxious Crowd,
Ah! from the Soul itself must issue forth
A Light, a Glory, and a luminous Cloud
    Enveloping the Earth!
And from the Soul itself must there be sent   305
A sweet & potent Voice, of it's own Birth,
Of all sweet Sounds the Life & Element.

O pure of Heart! thou need'st not ask of me
What this strong music in the Soul may be,
    What, & wherein it doth exist,   310
This light, this Glory, this fair luminous Mist,
This beautiful & beauty-making Power!
JOY, innocent Sara! Joy, that ne'er was given
Save to the Pure, & in their purest Hour,
JOY, Sara! is the Spirit & the Power,   315
That wedding Nature to us gives in Dower
    A new Earth & new Heaven
Undreamt of by the Sensual & the Proud!
Joy is that strong Voice, Joy that luminous Cloud –
    We, we ourselves rejoice!   320
And thence flows all that charms or ear or sight,
All melodies the Echoes of that Voice,
All Colors a Suffusion of that Light.

Sister & Friend of my devoutest Choice!
Thou being innocent & full of love,   325
And nested with the Darlings of thy Love,
And feeling in thy Soul, Heart, Lips & Arms
Even what the conjugal & mother Dove

That borrows genial Warmth from those, she warms,
Feels in her thrill'd wings, blessedly outspread –   330
Thou free'd awhile from Cares & human Dread
By the Immenseness of the Good & Fair
   Which thou see'st every where –
Thus, thus should'st thou rejoice!
To thee would all Things live from Pole to Pole,   335
Their Life the Eddying of thy living Soul. –
O dear! O Innocent! O full of love!
A very Friend! A Sister of my Choice –
O dear, as Light & Impulse from above,
Thus may'st thou ever, evermore rejoice!   340

                             S.T.C.

Hymn Before Sun-Rise, in the Vale of Chamouni

After the German of Friederike Brun[1]

Besides the Rivers, Arve and Arveiron, which have their sources in the foot of Mont Blanc, five conspicuous torrents rush down its sides; and within a few paces of the Glaciers, the Gentiana Major grows in immense numbers, with its 'flowers of loveliest blue'.

   Hast thou a charm to stay the morning-star
   In his steep course? So long he seems to pause
   On thy bald awful head, O sovran BLANC,
   The Arve and Arveiron at thy base
   Rave ceaselessly; but thou, most awful Form!   5
   Risest from forth thy silent sea of pines,
   How silently! Around thee and above

[1] Friederike Brun's 'Chamouny beym Sonnenaufgange' runs to no more than 20 lines, but in Coleridge's original printing he also used her notes without acknowledgement for a long prose preface.

Deep is the air and dark, substantial, black,
An ebon mass: methinks thou piercest it,
As with a wedge! But when I look again,   10
It is thine own calm home, thy crystal shrine,
Thy habitation from eternity!
O dread and silent Mount! I gazed upon thee,
Till thou, still present to the bodily sense,
Didst vanish from my thought: entranced in prayer   15
I worshipped the Invisible alone.

  Yet, like some sweet beguiling melody,
So sweet, we know not we are listening to it,
Thou, the meanwhile, wast blending with my Thought,
Yea, with my Life and Life's own secret joy: 20
Till the dilating Soul, enrapt, transfused,
Into the mighty vision passing – there
As in her natural form, swelled vast to Heaven!

  Awake, my soul! not only passive praise
Thou owest! not alone these swelling tears,   25
Mute thanks and secret ecstasy! Awake,
Voice of sweet song! Awake, my Heart, awake!
Green vales and icy cliffs, all join my Hymn.

  Thou first and chief, sole sovereign of the Vale!
O struggling with the darkness all the night,   30
And visited all night by troops of stars,
Or when they climb the sky or when they sink:
Companion of the morning-star at dawn,
Thyself Earth's rosy star, and of the dawn
Co-herald: wake, O wake, and utter praise!   35
Who sank thy sunless pillars deep in Earth?
Who filled thy countenance with rosy light?
Who made thee parent of perpetual streams?

  And you, ye five wild torrents fiercely glad!
Who called you forth from night and utter death,   40
From dark and icy caverns called you forth,
Down those precipitous, black, jaggéd rocks,
For ever shattered and the same for ever?

Who gave you your invulnerable life,
Your strength, your speed, your fury, and your joy,   45
Unceasing thunder and eternal foam?
And who commanded (and the silence came),
Here let the billows stiffen, and have rest?

Ye Ice-falls! ye that from the mountain's brow
Adown enormous ravines slope amain –   50
Torrents, methinks, that heard a mighty voice,
And stopped at once amid their maddest plunge!
Motionless torrents! silent cataracts!
Who made you glorious as the Gates of Heaven
Beneath the keen full moon? Who bade the sun   55
Clothe you with rainbows? Who, with living flowers
Of loveliest blue, spread garlands at your feet? –
GOD! let the torrents, like a shout of nations,
Answer! and let the ice-plains echo, GOD!
GOD! sing ye meadow-streams with gladsome voice!   60
Ye pine-groves, with your soft and soul-like sounds!
And they too have a voice, yon piles of snow,
And in their perilous fall shall thunder, GOD!

Ye living flowers that skirt the eternal frost!
Ye wild goats sporting round the eagle's nest!   65
Ye eagles, play-mates of the mountain-storm!
Ye lightnings, the dread arrows of the clouds!
Ye signs and wonders of the element!
Utter forth God, and fill the hills with praise!

Thou too, hoar Mount! with thy sky-pointing peaks,   70
Oft from whose feet the avalanche, unheard,
Shoots downward, glittering through the pure serene
Into the depth of clouds, that veil thy breast –
Thou too again, stupendous Mountain! thou
That as I raise my head, awhile bowed low   75
In adoration, upward from thy base
Slow travelling with dim eyes suffused with tears,
Solemnly seemest, like a vapoury cloud,
To rise before me – Rise, O ever rise,
Rise like a cloud of incense, from the Earth!   80

Thou kingly Spirit throned among the hills,
Thou dread ambassador from Earth to Heaven.
Great Hierarch! tell thou the silent sky,
And tell the stars, and tell yon rising sun
Earth, with her thousand voices, praises GOD.   85

The Pains of Sleep

Ere on my bed my limbs I lay,
It hath not been my use to pray,
With moving lips or bended knees;
But silently, by slow degrees,
My spirit I to Love compose,   5
In humble trust mine eye-lids close,
With reverential resignation,
No wish conceived, no thought exprest,
Only a sense of supplication;
A sense o'er all my soul imprest   10
That I am weak, yet not unblest,
Since in me, round me, every where
Eternal Strength and Wisdom are.

But yester-night I prayed aloud
In anguish and in agony,   15
Up-starting from the fiendish crowd
Of shapes and thoughts that tortured me:
A lurid light, a trampling throng,
Sense of intolerable wrong,
And whom I scorned, those only strong!   20
Thirst of revenge, the powerless will
Still baffled, and yet burning still!
Desire with loathing strangely mixed
On wild or hateful objects fixed.
Fantastic passions! maddening brawl!   25
And shame and terror over all!
Deeds to be hid which were not hid,

Which all confused I could not know,
Whether I suffered, or I did:
For all seemed guilt, remorse or woe,   30
My own or others still the same
Life-stifling fear, soul-stifling shame.
So two nights passed: the night's dismay
Saddened and stunned the coming day.
Sleep, the wide blessing, seemed to me   35
Distemper's worst calamity.
The third night, when my own loud scream
Had waked me from the fiendish dream,
O'ercome with sufferings strange and wild,
I wept as I had been a child;   40
And having thus by tears subdued
My anguish to a milder mood,
Such punishments, I said, were due
To natures deepliest stained with sin, –
For aye entempesting anew   45
The unfathomable hell within,
The horror of their deeds to view,
To know and loathe, yet wish and do!
Such griefs with such men well agree,
But wherefore, wherefore fall on me?   50
To be beloved is all I need,
And whom I love, I love indeed.

Phantom

All Look or Likeness caught from Earth,
All accident of Kin or Birth,
Had pass'd Away: there seem'd no Trace
Of Aught upon her brighten'd Face
Uprais'd beneath the rifted Stone,   5
Save of one Spirit, all her own/
She, she herself, and only she
Shone in her body visibly.

Constancy to an Ideal Object

Since all that beat about in Nature's range,
Or veer or vanish; why should'st thou remain
The only constant in a world of change,
O yearning THOUGHT! that liv'st but in the brain?
Call to the HOURS, that in the distance play,   5
The faery people of the future day –
Fond THOUGHT! not one of all that shining swarm
Will breathe on *thee* with life-enkindling breath,
Till when, like strangers shelt'ring from a storm,
Hope and Despair meet in the porch of Death!   10
Yet still thou haunt'st me; and though well I see,
She is not thou, and only thou art she,
Still, still as though some dear *embodied* Good,
Some *living* Love before my eyes there stood
With answering look a ready ear to lend,   15
I mourn to thee and say – 'Ah! loveliest Friend!
That this the meed of all my toils might be,
To have a home, an English home, and thee!'
Vain repetition! Home and Thou are one.
The peacefull'st cot, the moon shall shine upon,   20
Lulled by the Thrush and wakened by the Lark,
Without thee were but a becalméd bark,
Whose Helmsman on an ocean waste and wide
Sits mute and pale his mouldering helm beside.

And art thou nothing? Such thou art, as when   25
The woodman winding westward up the glen
At wintry dawn, where o'er the sheep-track's maze
The viewless snow-mist weaves a glist'ning haze,
Sees full before him, gliding without tread,
An image[1] with a glory round its head;   30

[1] This phenomenon, which the Author has himself experienced, and of which

The enamoured rustic worships its fair hues,
Nor knows he *makes* the shadow, he pursues!

[The Indifference of the Heavens]

What never is but only is to be
This is not Life –
O Hopeless Hope, and Death's Hypocrisy!
And with perpetual Promise, breaks its Promises. –

The Stars that wont to start, as on a chase,[1]   5
And twinkling insult on Heaven's darkened Face,
Like a conven'd Conspiracy of Spies
Wink at each other with confiding eyes,
Turn from the portent, all is blank on high,
No constellations alphabet the Sky –   10
The Heavens one large black Letter only shews,
And as a Child beneath its master's Blows
Shrills out at once its Task and its Affright,
The groaning world now learns to read aright,
And with its Voice of Voices cries out, O!   15

the reader may find a description in one of the earlier volumes of the *Manchester Philosophical Transactions*, is applied figuratively in the following passage of the *Aids to Reflection*:–

'Pindar's fine remark respecting the different effects of Music, on different characters, holds equally true of Genius – as many as are not delighted by it are disturbed, perplexed, irritated. The beholder either recognizes it as a projected form of his own Being, that moves before him with a Glory round its head, or recoils from it as a Spectre.' – *Aids to Reflection* [1825], p. 220. [S.T.C.]

[1] The last 11 lines were extracted and published separately by E.H.C. under the title 'Coeli enarrant' ['The heavens are telling': see Psalm xix]. They are based by Coleridge on a childhood memory of an occasion when he was punished so hard by his father in the schoolroom that instead of the required lesson he could only cry 'O!'

Recollections of Love

I

How warm this woodland wild Recess!
  Love surely hath been breathing here;
  And this sweet bed of heath, my dear!
Swells up, then sinks with fair caress,
  As if to have you yet more near.   5

II

Eight springs have flown, since last I lay
  On sea-ward Quantock's heathy hills,
  Where quiet sounds from hidden rills
Float here and there, like things astray,
  And high o'er head the sky-lark shrills.   10

III

No voice as yet had made the air
  Be music with your name; yet why
  That asking look? that yearning sigh?
That sense of promise every where?
  Belovéd! flew your spirit by?   15

IV

As when a mother doth explore
  The rose-mark on her long-lost child,
  I met, I loved you, maiden mild!
As whom I long had loved before –
  So deeply had I been beguiled.   20

V

You stood before me like a thought,
  A dream remembered in a dream.
  But when those meek eyes first did seem
To tell me, Love within you wrought –
  O Greta, dear domestic stream!   25

VI

Has not, since then, Love's prompture deep,

> Has not Love's whisper evermore
> Been ceaseless, as thy gentle roar?
> Sole voice, when other voices sleep,
> Dear under-song in Clamor's hour.   30

A Tombless Epitaph[1]

'Tis true, Idoloclastes Satyrane!
(So call him, for so mingling blame with praise,
And smiles with anxious looks, his earliest friends,
Masking his birth-name, wont to character
His wild-wood fancy and impetuous zeal,)   5
'Tis true that, passionate for ancient truths,
And honouring with religious love the Great
Of elder times, he hated to excess,
With an unquiet and intolerant scorn,
The hollow Puppets of a hollow Age,   10
Ever idolatrous, and changing ever
Its worthless Idols! Learning, Power, and Time,
(Too much of all) thus wasting in vain war
Of fervid colloquy. Sickness, 'tis true,
Whole years of weary days, besieged him close,   15
Even to the gates and inlets of his life!
But it is true, no less, that strenuous, firm,
And with a natural gladness, he maintained
The citadel unconquered, and in joy
Was strong to follow the delightful Muse.   20
For not a hidden path, that to the shades
Of the beloved Parnassian forest leads,
Lurked undiscovered by him; not a rill
There issues from the fount of Hippocrene,
But he had traced it upward to its source,   25
Through open glade, dark glen, and secret dell,
Knew the gay wild flowers on its banks, and culled
Its med'cinable herbs. Yea, oft alone,
Piercing the long-neglected holy cave,

[1] Imitated, though in the movements rather than the thoughts, from the viith of *Gli Epitafi* of Chiabrera. [S.T.C.]

The haunt obscure of old Philosophy,   30
He bade with lifted torch its starry walls
Sparkle, as erst they sparkled to the flame
Of odorous lamps tended by Saint and Sage.
O framed for calmer times and nobler hearts!
O studious Poet, eloquent for truth!   35
Philosopher! contemning wealth and death,
Yet docile, childlike, full of Life and Love!
Here, rather than on monumental stone,
This record of thy worth thy Friend inscribes,
Thoughtful, with quiet tears upon his cheek.   40

Limbo[1]

Tis a strange Place, this Limbo! not a Place,
Yet name it so – where Time & weary Space
Fetter'd from flight, with night-mair sense of Fleeing
Strive for their last crepuscular Half-being –
Lank Space, and scytheless Time with branny Hands   5
Barren and soundless as the measuring Sands,
Mark'd but by Flit of Shades – unmeaning they
As Moonlight on the Dial of the Day –
But that is lovely – looks like Human Time,
An old Man with a steady Look sublime   10
That stops his earthly Task to watch the Skies –
But he is blind – a statue hath such Eyes –
Yet having moon-ward turn'd his face by chance –
Gazes the orb with moon-like Countenance
With scant white hairs, with fore-top bald & high   15
He gazes still, his eyeless Face all Eye –
As twere an Organ full of silent Sight
His whole Face seemeth to rejoice in Light/
Lip touching Lip, all moveless, Bust and Limb,

[1] There seem to be echoes of Donne here: 'Hell is but privation / Of him' in 'To Mr T. W.' [K.C.] and the 'dull privations' of the 'Nocturnall upon St Lucies Day'. [Ed.]

He seems to gaze at that which seems to gaze on Him!   20

No such sweet Sights doth Limbo Den immure,
Wall'd round and made a Spirit-jail secure
By the mere Horror of blank Nought at all –
Whose circumambience doth these Ghosts enthrall.
A lurid Thought is growthless dull Privation,   25
But the Hag, Madness, scalds the Fiends of Hell
With frenzy-dreams, all incompassible
Of aye-unepithetable Negation

A lurid thought is growthless dull Privation
Yet that is but a Purgatory Curse   30
Hell knows a fear far worse,
A fear, a future fate. Tis *positive Negation!*

[From ms.]

Song

From *Zapolya* (Act II, Scene I, ll. 65–80)

A sunny shaft did I behold,
  From sky to earth it slanted:
And poised therein a bird so bold –
  Sweet bird, thou were enchanted!

He sank, he rose, he twinkled, he trolled   5
  Within that shaft of sunny mist;
His eyes of fire, his beak of gold,
  All else of amethyst!

And thus he sang: 'Adieu! adieu!
Love's dreams prove seldom true.   10
The blossoms they make no delay:
The sparkling dew-drops will not stay.
  Sweet month of May,
    We must away;
      Far, far away!   15
            Today! today!'

Work Without Hope

Lines composed 21st February 1825

All Nature seems at work. Slugs leave their lair –
The bees are stirring – birds are on the wing –
And Winter slumbering in the open air,
Wears on his smiling face a dream of Spring!
And I, the while, the sole unbusy thing,   5
Nor honey make, nor pair, nor build, nor sing.

Yet well I ken the banks where amaranths blow,
Have traced the fount whence streams of nectar flow.
Bloom, O ye amaranths! bloom for whom ye may,
For me ye bloom not! Glide, rich streams, away!   10
With lips unbrightened, wreathless brow, I stroll:
And would you learn the spells that drowse my soul?
Work without Hope draws nectar in a sieve,
And Hope without an object cannot live.

The Pang More Sharp Than All

An Allegory

I

He too has flitted from his secret nest,
Hope's last and dearest child without a name! –
Has flitted from me, like the warmthless flame,
That makes false promise of a place of rest
To the tired Pilgrim's still believing mind; –   5
Or like some Elfin Knight in kingly court,
Who having won all guerdons in his sport,
Glides out of view, and whither none can find!

II

Yes! he hath flitted from me – with what aim,
Or why, I know not! 'Twas a home of bliss,   10
And he was innocent, as the pretty shame
Of babe, that tempts and shuns the menaced kiss,
From its twy-cluster'd hiding place of snow!
Pure as the babe, I ween, and all aglow
As the dear hopes, that swell the mother's breast –   15
Her eyes down gazing o'er her claspéd charge; –
Yet gay as that twice happy father's kiss,
That well might glance aside, yet never miss,
Where the sweet mark emboss'd so sweet a targe –
Twice wretched he who hath been doubly blest!   20

III

Like a loose blossom on a gusty night
He flitted from me – and has left behind
(As if to them his faith he ne'er did plight)
Of either sex and answerable mind
Two playmates, twin-births of his foster-dame: –   25
The one a steady lad (Esteem he hight)
And Kindness is the gentler sister's name.
Dim likeness now, though fair she be and good,
Of that bright Boy who hath us all forsook; –
But in his full-eyed aspect when she stood,   30
And while her face reflected every look,
And in reflection kindled – she became
So like Him, that almost she seem'd the same!

IV

Ah! he is gone, and yet will not depart! –
Is with me still, yet I from him exiled!   35
For still there lives within my secret heart
The magic image of the magic Child,
Which there he made up-grow by his strong art,
As in that crystal[1] orb – wise Merlin's feat, –
The wondrous 'World of Glass', wherein inisled   40
All long'd for things their beings did repeat; –

---

[1] *Faerie Queene*, b. III, c 2, s. 19. [S.T.C.]

And there he left it, like a Sylph beguiled,
To live and yearn and languish incomplete!

V

Can wit of man a heavier grief reveal?
Can sharper pang from hate or scorn arise? –   45
Yes! one more sharp there is that deeper lies,
Which fond Esteem but mocks when he would heal.
Yet neither scorn nor hate did it devise,
But sad compassion and atoning zeal!
One pang more blighting-keen than hope betray'd!   50
And this it is my woful hap to feel,
When, at her Brother's hest, the twin-born Maid
With face averted and unsteady eyes,
Her truant playmate's faded robe puts on;
And inly shrinking from her own disguise   55
Enacts the faery Boy that's lost and gone.
O worse than all! O pang all pangs above
Is Kindness counterfeiting absent Love!

Song

Though veiled in spires of myrtle wreath,
Love is a sword that cuts its sheath,
And through the clefts, itself has made,
We spy the flashes of the blade!

But through the clefts, itself has made,   5
We likewise see Love's flashing blade
By rust consumed or snapt in twain:
And only hilt and stump remain.

Love's Apparition and Evanishment

An Allegoric Romance

    Like a lone Arab, old and blind,
    Some caravan had left behind,
    Who sits beside a ruin'd well,
    Where the shy sand-asps bask and swell;
And now he hangs his agéd head aslant,   5
And listens for a human sound – in vain!
And now the aid, which Heaven alone can grant,
Upturns his eyeless face from Heaven to gain; –
Even thus, in vacant mood, one sultry hour,
Resting my eye upon a drooping plant,   10
With brow low-bent, within my garden-bower,
I sate upon the couch of camomile;
And – whether 'twas a transient sleep, perchance,
Flitted across the idle brain, the while
I watch'd the sickly calm with aimless scope,   15
In my own heart; or that, indeed a trance,
Turn'd my eye inward – thee, O genial Hope,
Love's elder sister! thee did I behold,
Drest as a bridesmaid, but all pale and cold,
With roseless cheek, all pale and cold and dim,   20
    Lie lifeless at my feet!
And then came Love, a sylph in bridal trim,
    And stood beside my seat;
She bent, and kiss'd her sister's lips,
    As she was wont to do; –   25
Alas! 'twas but a chilling breath
Woke just enough of life in death
    To make Hope die anew.
L'ENVOY

In vain we supplicate the Powers above;
There is no resurrection for the Love   30
That, nursed in tenderest care, yet fades away
In the chill'd heart by gradual self-decay.

Epitaph

Stop, Christian passer-by! – Stop, child of God,
And read with gentle breast. Beneath this sod
A poet lies, or that which once seem'd he. –
O, lift one thought in prayer for S.T.C.;
That he who many a year with toil of breath   5
Found death in life, may here find life in death!
Mercy for praise – to be forgiven for fame[1]
He ask'd, and hoped, through Christ. Do thou the same!

---

[1] 'N.6. – "for" in the sense of "instead of"' [S.T.C., letter]